To and Fro Children

A GUIDE TO SUCCESSFUL
PARENTING AFTER DIVORCE

JILL BURRETT

Thorsons
An Imprint of HarperCollinsPublishers

Thorsons
An Imprint of HarperCollins*Publishers*
77–85 Fulham Palace Road,
Hammersmith, London W6 8JB

Published in 1991 by Allen & Unwin Pty Ltd, 8 Napier Street,
North Sydney, NSW 2059 Australia
Published by Thorsons 1993
1   3   5   7   9   10   8   6   4   2

© Jill Burrett 1991, 1993

Jill Burrett asserts the moral right to
be identified as the author of this work

A catalogue record for this book
is available from the British Library

ISBN 0 7225 2794 2

Typeset by Harper Phototypesetters Limited,
Northampton, England
Printed in Great Britain by
HarperCollinsManufacturing Glasgow

CONTENTS

Acknowledgements   6
Foreword   7
Preface   9

1 IT'S UP TO YOU   11

   Parenting hopes and challenges   11
   The story of Doug and Anne   13
   Helpful and unhelpful attitudes   16
   Who this book is for   19
   Language and labels   19

2 PARTNERSHIPS, SEPARATIONS, NEW ATTITUDES   23

   Relationships and romance   23
   Expectations, disappointments, new challenges   25
   Separation, recovery, new insights   27
   Old partnerships over time   28
   Always a parent   30
   What the research says   32
   Why it's worth it   33
   Cultivating helpful attitudes   35

3 SUCCESSFUL TEAM PARENTING FROM DIFFERENT CAMPS   43

   Planning your children's two-household family   43
   Making it work   47
   When it's hard to talk to each other   51
   Some common concerns   51
   Fielding children's questions well   55
   Imaginary problems   56
   Are we getting there?   58
   Summary   59

4 MAKING THE MOST OF PART-TIME PARENTING   61

   In the beginning   61
   Getting into the swing of it   62
   Talking to your children   66
   Making good use of your time together   70
   Setting limits   72
   Including others   75
   When there's another 'father'   77
   Keeping going   77

5 STEP-FAMILIES   79

   New partnerships and good timing   80
   Making it known   82
   The special challenges   83
   Who should be responsible for what   86
   Making room for everybody   88
   What should we call ourselves?   89
   A new baby   91
   Grandparents   92
   Positive attitudes for successful step-families 93

6 PART-TIME STEP-PARENTS   97

   Contemplating a 'package deal'   97
   Getting started as a step-mother   99
   Helping everyone get on together   103
   Communication is vital   105
   How to feel more relaxed about it   106
   Seeing rewards for your efforts   109

7 MAINTAINING AUTHORITY   111

   Whatever happened to parental authority?   112
   Why have rules at all?   113
   Authoritative parenting   114
   What do we want from our children?   114
   What happens when authority gets lost   115

How to stay in charge   120
Golden rules for staying in charge   128

8 UNDERSTANDING CHILDREN AND DIVORCE   129

Children and breakups   129
Could they be seriously troubled?   132
Resilience and vulnerability   134
Tuning in to children   137
Talking about fault, truth and feelings   142

9 REFLECTIONS   147

Changes begin with positive thinking   147
When there's no answer   149
Acceptance   151
Having doubts   151
Being realistic about parenting   152
Taking care of yourself   154
Epilogue   155

Index   157

ACKNOWLEDGEMENTS

To the many clients who have come to me for practical and rational advice about separation and afterwards, making me realise that this book needed to be written.

To my husband's son, whose apparently easy-going acceptance of his family circumstances has often been an inspiration to me.

To his father, whose acceptance of the 'loss' of his son taught me a lot about how this can best be done, if it has to happen, and about how often compromising is worthwhile.

J.B.

FOREWORD

Family life is changing. Being a parent has never been easy but it seems we are making it more and more difficult for ourselves. The majority of parents now have jobs outside the home and are trying to balance the responsibility of work and family. At the same time, a significant proportion of parents have no paid work at all and are struggling with poverty and family life. As marriage has become more of an emotional partnership, many couples have found it harder to combine being partners with being parents. Marriage is decreasing; divorce is increasing. Family life appears to be under pressure from all directions.

On an average day in the United Kingdom about 500 children and young people will experience the separation or divorce of their parents. The Children Act 1989, implemented in 1991, stresses that 'parents are forever'. The Act encourages parents who are living apart to plan together how they will share the care of their children when living in those two different households. Family life rarely remains static. Not only do children grow and have new and changing needs but the adults also build new lives. Within five years half those separated and divorced parents will have new partners and remarried. The children having adjusted to being part of two lone parent households will now become members of one or maybe two stepfamilies.

We do not know how many children are moving to and fro between their mother's home and their father's home on a regular basis. Most children do stay in touch with the parent who has moved out over the first few years. For some this may be regular visits every fortnight, for others contact is only in the school holidays. Sadly, five years after the divorce over half the children have lost all contact with that parent. Being a part-time parent is particularly difficult.

This book is very much about positive parenting – whether you are doing it full-time or part-time, as a parent or a step-parent. The focus is successful parenting after divorce because that event forces parents to consider how they are going to share the care of their children. As Jill Burrett points out, sharing the care of our children is not unusual – many of us share our children with grandparents, friends, neighbours, child carers, teachers and others. The difference here is sharing the care with your ex-partner from two different parental households; sharing the care of your child with someone you have already found you can no longer live with. For many it also means sharing the

7

care with a new partner, who may have no experience of children at all, or who may bring his or her own children into the stepfamily, and may be unsure of his or her role with your children.

Given the current public debate about parental responsibilities and the variety of family households in which children today are growing up, this book is very timely. The advice and guidance on authoritative parenting, on the importance of consistency, good team management and basic planning for the family would be invaluable to any parent, whatever their marital or domestic status. Some of the tips for part-time parents are just as applicable to that growing band of fathers having to work away from home during the week who are also becoming weekend fathers. Parents who are both out working will identify with the urge to give in to children because the time you spend with them is precious and you don't want to be nagging or correcting them all the time, and those with childminders and other child carers will understand children's anxieties about leaving one carer for the other, moving from one familiar household or setting to another where the rules or expectations may be slightly different.

The book is also at pains to point out the importance of balance, between the needs of adults and the needs of children. Recent research has highlighted the impact that a new baby and children can have on marriage. A couple may grow apart unless they invest in their relationship as much as they do in their children and family life. With one in two remarriages ending in divorce compared with one in three first marriages, this is a very critical consideration if we are to prevent even further disruption for children if the stepfamily breaks down.

During the 1990s it is estimated that between 2.5 and 3 million children will spend part of their childhood growing up in a two parent family, then a lone parent family and then a stepfamily. Understanding the challenges of effective post-divorce parenting and shared parenting in stepfamilies is essential to help children through the various changes and adjustments they have to make during those changes in their family life. This book highlights the fact, made clear from research, that conflict between parents makes it more difficult for children to adjust. Children do need contact with both their parents even if it is difficult and painful for the adults. Children can cope with moving between two households if the adults are prepared to be honest and open with them about what is happening, do not ask the children to make decisions about where they should live, and ensure the children feel wanted and part of both households.

Differences and conflicts are inevitable in family life. Children go through various stages of testing their parents as they learn to become more independent. Children need to feel loved, safe and secure. Jill Burrett's golden rules for staying in charge should be on every family's kitchen door. The fifth golden rule, 'proceed with confidence', could become the motto for all parents and step-parents who read this book.

PREFACE

Any parent who has been through a separation, as well as any welfare professional involved in assisting parents and children with the necessary adjustments, has long been aware of the good sense in being cooperative and unembittered for the children's benefit. They will have perceived the worth of working to sustain a child's relationship with both their father and mother after a separation. In embarking on this project, I was also aware of the need to foster a more positive, flexible, easygoing, 'normal' and optimistic attitude on the part of separating parents; I wanted to issue a challenge to parents to use the regrettable but unchangeable event of divorce to reappraise their role as parents in useful ways.

Not so long after this book was first published, I became involved in an assignment which required me to familiarise myself thoroughly with the new Children Act which was to come into effect in October 1991. In particular, I studied those parts of it which deal specifically with the legal side of separation, divorce and children. I found that the central philosophy of self-help and commitment to nurturing family relationships after separation that this book proclaims is prominently reflected in the new Act's terms and provisions.

The Children Act (1989) re-emphasises the importance and indeed the superiority of the family as the medium which best meets a child's developmental needs. It encourages commitment to joint parental responsibility after a separation – yes, mothers *and* fathers – as well as specifically stating that state intervention into parenting responsibilities and legal methods for solving family disputes associated with divorce should be only used as last resorts.

This could not be a more clear statement that not only are children's to and fro relationships after divorce to be nurtured and valued, but also that parents should be encouraged and assisted to acquire the necessary insight and vision to manage their parenting responsibly and cooperatively.

Our new child welfare laws therefore represent a most timely endorsement of the usefulness of a book specifically about independent, positive post-divorce parenting.

J.B. January 1993

1

It's Up to You

This is a guide to parenting successfully from two separate households after a divorce, so your children can thrive. Some people call this to and fro way of being with separated parents 'access', or 'contact'.

It's a book which in some ways is a philosophy as well as a guide, in the sense that it's about looking forwards, getting on with life, improving your performance through growth and change. It's about applying this approach to life to the job we often forget is our most important one, the one which can have the most far-reaching consequences of anything we do – caring for our children.

Parenting hopes and challenges

Every parent wants to be a successful one. We invest our children with the potential to achieve everything we'd like to have achieved ourselves. We try (often consciously) to improve our parenting in all those areas where we feel our own parents were lacking, and to provide our children with all those things we value about our own childhood. Many of us who are separated want to make sure our children don't suffer from their parents' divorce the way we ourselves suffered because our own parents didn't stay together. We worry quite a lot of the time about the effect our separation will have or is having on our children, and want to do all we can to make up for the changes that they've had to make and the relationships they've had to accept. And most of us who divorce want to ensure

11

our children don't miss out on all that matters about having parents whose marriage worked.

There's not much doubt that divorce is a sad and disrupting experience for children, but they usually get over it in time and will certainly do so faster if you handle it well. Your children need to continue feeling they belong and are important to both their parents, just as they have always done, so that they have the confidence to benefit from the reorganisation of their family.

This book is about approaching life and its challenges head on, so you can make the most out of something that didn't work out the way it was meant to, something that can't be left behind, forgotten, or set aside, because of your children. It's about cultivating a positive and flexible approach to family life in response to a disappointing but necessary change; about learning that to dwell on past failures and current frustrations is only useful to the point where a new insight is gained, leading to a new and effective policy being devised and used successfully. It's about looking ahead in positive ways for possible problems so you can avoid them or at least be ready for them.

Parenthood is challenging enough anyway, without the shadow of a past disappointment adding an extra dimension to the joys and the demands of having children. When you separate you have to review entirely the basis of your role as parents, and 'start over'. Being parents but separated is different and takes some adjusting to, especially when you take on new relationships and become part of a step-family. Most of us just muddle along managing reasonably well, crossing the various bridges as we come to them, only realising the full complexities (and the hazards) of reorganised families as we go along or as we look back on things. Many parents say they felt they were very much 'going it alone' and would have liked good advice early on about separation, remarriage and step-relations. If you can learn to approach separate parenting in a realistic, lighthearted and positive way, anticipating and adapting to the extra dimensions in your family, and seeing it as a challenge rather than a hassle, you'll find it all much easier and happier for everyone.

The story of Doug and Anne

I used to rather resent it that Doug seemed so keen to see the children as often as he could, when I thought he'd spent no time at all with them when we were together. And they'd come home excited and disobedient on Sunday nights, telling me about all the money he'd spent on them and how he was going to buy them each a bike, and take them overseas with him next year, etc., etc. I'd be left with having to settle them down on Mondays for school, sort out all their dirty and sometimes missing clothes; they'd be irritable all day Monday. I'd end up wondering if he was looking after them properly, the state they seemed to be in after they got back each time. At times, when I was feeling particularly low, which now I realise was usually when I was on my own and tired, I used to get resentful that he seemed to have all the happy, leisured times with the children, while I was stuck with the weekday grind of getting to school, making sure homework got done, always having to be on at them to get something done, be somewhere on time. All this and getting to work myself. And the weekends did seem lonely. Having the house quiet took a lot of getting used to.

It wasn't until much, much later, that I began to see that my resentment about Doug and his relationship with the children was really me still getting over the fact that we'd separated. We'd both more or less agreed that we'd have to live separate lives, but I didn't realise how long after we did part, that my feelings about him would still be changing so much from week to week as I got used to the disappointment, hurt and rage I was feeling, and the sense of failure about myself.

Eventually I realised that part of the reason I resented him apparently wanting to spend so much time with them was actually me not looking forward to being without them myself, worrying that the more time they were with him, the more they might come to have a stronger relationship with him than with me, what with all those promises of bikes and trips which I couldn't offer them. And I was feeling angry that he obviously hadn't been able to have fun with them with me around because our relationship cramped his style. It must have been really hard for him to cope with only seeing the boys every other weekend and feeling cut off from them, and no wonder he wanted to do extra exciting things with them, but I certainly couldn't see it this way at the time.

Looking back now on that time straight after we separated, and for about the next year and a half even, I feel grateful to my children for coping so well with having to adjust to separate relationships with both their parents. I certainly can't have made it easier for them, caught up as I was with my own emotional state, which must have shown itself to them and affected their freedom to enjoy their father, even though I thought I was being pretty careful about this. Although it took longer than we both thought it would to get over each other, I know I've learnt a lot of useful things from having divorced and I even feel I'm a better parent for it.

Doug's version of events during the period straight after his separation from Anne shows how very different two parents' views often are in relation to the same children, the same family, even though both of them in their own ways try to put the children first:

I had been worrying for months, even years, about how I'd be able to be a proper father if our marriage didn't work out, and how I'd live with the children's disappointment that their family broke up. I really worried that they'd feel

I'd abandoned them because they stayed with their mother in the home we'd had together. So I tried really hard to see them as often as I could so they'd be reassured of my continued love for them and be able to feel that family life was continuing even though a bit differently now.

I think Annie found it hard initially to accept my motives for being with the children. Picking them up and returning them meant that we saw each other often and while we were both trying hard to be civilised, these meetings tended to mean old feelings surfaced, bad ones as well as good ones. I think she tended to judge my competence with the children by how much time I'd spent with them when we were together, which wasn't much I admit during the last few years. It certainly wasn't easy getting the visiting thing going. It seemed very artificial for all of us to start with, and I didn't realise how constant children can be when you're looking after them solo! I think I kept providing them with activities and treats to keep them interested in coming, and because it was such a pleasure to see them after an absence that I wanted to celebrate and make a fuss of them. Annie kept on giving me details about their needs which seemed obvious to me, and it made me feel she didn't trust me with them. I was probably really annoying too, because I think she really didn't want to separate as much as I did and seeing me all the time over the children would have affected how quickly she got over it all, I guess.

The kids and I have lots of fun together and now we're all much more easy-going about everything, doing ordinary everyday things which give us more time for talking and relaxing. I guess I'm more confident about my relationship with them than I was to start with. I think it's a good sign that they seem to be able to talk a bit about Mum and her new man. They took a while to get used to my lady friend, but now they've accepted her, their visits are a lot easier. Sometimes I feel I'll never get really close to them, not being part of their everyday lives. I don't think I'm able to influence the way they're growing up as much as I'd like to. But it's going really well most of the time, and in many ways I'm more of a parent than I would have been if we'd stayed together.

Doug and Anne are both parents who found it hard after their separation but have learnt a fair bit about themselves through the efforts they've made. Now they can look back and see the contribution they were each making to how the children were managing in a way that's sympathetic to the other's viewpoint and is accepting of it, though they haven't always been able to do this. The things that niggled them about each other are commonplace, so maybe some bits of their story are familiar to you. *Appreciating one another's point of view is an important step towards successful co-parenting. Once you can do this in relation to each other, most of your problems with parenting across two households will be over, because you trust each other enough to really communicate.* But even when you can communicate fairly well over the children, you'll find that the sort of 'parallel' parenting that being separated involves presents some challenges you mightn't have anticipated.

Helpful and unhelpful attitudes

This book encourages you to rethink the usual view of separation and divorce. You'll have to put aside assumptions about the trauma of broken homes, psychological damage to children, the emotional poverty of one-parent families and the many other negative stereotypes associated with marriage failure. *You'll have to dispense with notions of blameworthiness, justice, fairness, rights, fault and deservingness, and learn to understand these factors in terms of how they influence people's attitudes and behaviour – and hence relationships – in unhelpful ways.* You'll need to take on board a commitment to self-responsibility, personal awareness, insight about relationships, and the potential for growth and change in people's lives. Being self-aware means you can be one step ahead in avoiding family pressures, solving them effectively when they do arise, because you feel in charge of your life.

To do this you need to acquire the ability to accept the painful, destructive and self-absorbing feelings of a failed relationship and put them in perspective, so you'll be able to use the disappointment of your separation as something positive in your life. You need to see it as an event which taught you something useful about yourself, your life and your partnerships, and helped you grow and change in useful ways; something which gave you the impetus to become a really successful parent because the extra challenges of living apart from your mate made you even more determined to get it right. You need to rethink your relationship with your 'ex' and change from being a former lover to a successful co-parent, detached from your emotional past as partners, and getting on with life. *You can do a lot to make it a happy and enriching thing for your children to belong to two households, and become a more effective parent than you might ever have been without the extra challenges of family life after divorce.*

Most of the skills and attitudes which make for happy 'post-divorce' family relationships are the same as those which make for effective parenting in any family. Combine these with what you have been able to learn from your marriage experience even though it didn't last, and you can achieve the insight necessary to avoid contributing to the difficulties that are bound to crop up. And you can laugh at yourself as you progress past each challenge, sharing the funny side of life with your family and friends, showing how a sense of humour can help people feel more relaxed and easy-going because it reduces tensions, including family tensions, so well.

Divorce, remarriage and 'blended' families are so common that it is a mistake to cling to a notion of the ideal, intact family as if anything short of one is second best. Mistaken in the sense that it helps no one to have their circumstances classified as second-rate.

Your family, and everyone else, will be on the lookout for problems and expecting disappointments.

Of course this doesn't mean we shouldn't hope for successful first marriages followed by happy lasting family life. Nor does it mean that we should abandon a less than ideal family life without serious and careful consideration of how it could be improved or adapted. All families have some problems from time to time. And if we're honest with ourselves, we'll admit that our children are demanding and unlikeable perhaps more of the time than we imagined they'd be, though we're not 'supposed to' feel this way about them! Children come between you and your partner and affect your relationship in subtle ways. With real effort and good humour family ups and downs and relationship problems can be overcome. Then you will have avoided the sadness and disappointment of a separation, feel proud of this achievement, and probably find you have enriched your marriage too.

Children are a very good reason for working hard at making a partnership work, but they're not usually a good enough reason on their own for keeping an unsatisfactory marriage going. Often separating and reorganising your family is a constructive step which improves everyone's lives, after all the necessary (and sometimes painful) adjustments have been made. So thinking of divorced parents and step-families as different and inferior isn't helpful. What is helpful is acknowledging the real human issues of family change, and getting on with life armed with new insights to apply to yourself and your relationships. Every experience in life, even the ones you could do without, can provide opportunities for give and take, possibilities for growth and change. You can use the events in your life, even those you didn't plan and which were a disappointment and presented problems, in such a way that you won't be held back for long by frustrations and annoyances. In this way you'll learn to change, grow, feel in charge of your life and have fun passing these successes on to your children.

Who this book is for

Whether you're on your own because of a breakup with someone you had children with, or you have a new partner and have begun family life again with children from either of your earlier relationships, this book is for you. In fact, it's for everyone directly involved, whether as a parent or a step-parent, with children who belong to two households and regularly spend time in each of them. If you're on your own and determined to stay that way, the odds are that in fact you won't, and nor will your 'ex'. So matters of remarriage and step-parenting are likely to concern at least one, if not both of you, at some point.

Whether you share the children equally time-wise, or they're with one of you most of the time and visit the other regularly (usually at weekends), you'll find chapters geared to your situation. *Understanding and appreciating other people's points of view, whether or not you actually sympathise with them, is fundamental to successfully managing relationships of all kinds.* So you stand to gain from the chapter on being a part-time parent even if you're with the children most of the time. And if you're on your own with the children and they visit your 'ex' and his new wife's children and their new child, then all their challenges concern you. Many of the most important issues fall into more than one subject area, and when this happens, they'll be addressed more than once to emphasise their importance.

Language and labels

Language and labels for the many relationships and inter-relationships of family life can be awkward. A parent who looks after their children for more of the time than the other parent is often known as the 'custodial parent', the one who has 'custody' or 'residence' or is the 'major caretaker'. This is the mother in most separated families. The part-time or visited parent, the one who has 'access' to or 'contact' with the children is usually the father. For simplicity then, we'll refer to the parent who looks after the children most of the time as the mother, and the visited parent as the father, although it's sometimes the other way round or shared equally. Instead of referring to your child's other parent as 'your former partner' or 'the other parent', we'll rather reluctantly use the word 'ex' for brevity, although this has a rather defunct and disparaging ring to it. This book is about your relationship with your mate from the past being the very opposite of defunct!

We'll avoid using the formal legal terms 'custody' or 'residence' and 'access' or 'contact', because this is a book about easy-going, cooperative parenting and not about formal rights, obligations and entitlements. Nor is it about sorting out family disagreements in law courts. The criminal associations of the word 'custody' hardly suit it to harmonizing family life. 'Access' means different things to different people, ranging from credit cards to computer information searches to prison visiting privileges, although separated parents frequently use it, for want of a better word, to mean the way in which their child conducts a relationship with a parent. The recent introduction (The Children Act 1989) of the terms 'residence' and 'contact' to replace 'custody' and 'access' is certainly an improvement. 'Divorce' is also really a legal term and many people don't get divorced for quite a long time after they separate, if ever. The event which is important for all the family relationships is the actual separation, and it's from this point on that all the adjusting has to begin. The divorce itself doesn't usually affect the children in the same way.

The words 'step-parent' and 'step-family' unfortunately have a rather second-rate or even negative ring to them, which reflects the often problematic nature of these relationships. The prefix 'step' is inaccurate anyway, having originated from an old word meaning deprived because of death, not because of a change of heart. But since we generally know what we mean by it, we'll continue to use it until we find a better word, one without the negative associations.

'Half-brother' or 'half-sister' is used to mean a sibling who has one parent in common with you. But they may at times feel much less than half as nice as a 'real' brother or sister, and sometimes feel twice as nice! Step-siblings of course are not even half related by blood even though they may have grown up together. You can see that in terms of the real nature and strength of relationships, there's an enormous number of variations possible which aren't really reflected in the titles we use. We still label people by their blood relationship to us or by the absence of one. In this book we'll aim to be clear and unambiguous, acknowledging the inadequacies of current labels.

Will some clever person come up with some warm-sounding, accurate names and titles which express relationships and positions in modern families, please? Meanwhile, read on!

2

Partnerships, Separations, New Attitudes

We often hear about the supposed decay of family life and contemporary pressures on relationships resulting in depressing divorce statistics. There almost seems to be a suggestion that we should be reviewing our assumptions about marriage and family life as we know it because modern living has made these fundamental institutions obsolete. Yet our culture is still pervaded by desirable images of fulfilling relationships, happy families and accomplished, healthy children, so we must be a long way from being ready to change these traditional aspirations, though there have been significant changes in the makeup and lifespan of families.

Relationships and romance

Making a commitment to a relationship is one of the most exciting and important decisions in our lives but we are, on the whole, inexperienced at making choices about lasting relationships. Many of us do not anticipate that beyond the 'honeymoon' period marriages need a mutual commitment to putting in effort. It would help if we appreciated better that passionate love must always turn into a sort of bonded companionship with time, and that having children takes a great deal of time, money and energy, which has to come from somewhere. At the time of our lives when most of us first make a commitment to another person, there are a great many pressures on us to become part of a couple, but we often aren't experienced, independent or confident enough to make a wise choice.

In some ways 'bonded companionship' does sound rather dull, though we hope to feel a deep sense of lasting commitment as thrilling in its way as being newly in love. Many people, however, find themselves unable to adapt to changes caused by the passage of time and the arrival of children, tending to blame the relationship itself for their dissatisfaction. They find it more difficult to make the necessary compromises and adjustments than they would if they had a more realistic idea of long-term partnerships and a better understanding of themselves in relationships. Perhaps they're expecting too much.

Yet marriage is as popular as ever. We pair up with the same romantic notions of effortless happiness, honest communication and assumed fidelity, naturally progressing to a cementing of the relationship through having children. We have the same expectations of lasting happiness that people have had for generations, despite contemporary marriage failure rates.

The emphasis we place on romantic love as the basis for selecting a mate has a lot to answer for. When you're newly 'in love', it doesn't seem as if the relationship needs any effort and attention, because the exciting and compelling 'chemistry' seems to make it feel as if everything will just take care of itself. It probably won't unless both of you are personally secure people who are sufficiently in touch with your individual needs and feelings to be able to communicate them trustingly from the start. Most of us don't know enough about how we perform and react in relationships, which makes it difficult to see what's really happening, and to communicate accurately with our partner. Many of us, quite without realising it, avoid the kind of honest exchanges with our new love either because deep down we are afraid they could threaten the pleasure we've found together, or because we aren't sufficiently in touch with ourselves. We make compromises about our real needs and feelings to ensure we remain loved, to preserve the security of the relationship, saying what we think our partner wants to hear and doing what we think will please. So the scene is set for communication to be less than ideal, leading to problems sooner or later.

If you're fortunate enough to have plenty of personal confidence and self-awareness, then your chances of having a relationship which satisfies you and which lasts are high. The key to successful relationships is acquiring an awareness of yourself, your impact on others, and the way others affect you. Learning to understand what really happened in your former marriage will help you become more self-aware, enabling you to manage your life after separation more effectively, improving your chances of a better relationship next time and, most importantly, ensuring your children end up enriched by your life changes rather than damaged by them.

Expectations, disappointments, new challenges

Divorce doesn't seem to discourage people from having a second try at creating a happy family, since the great majority of separated people form new partnerships. Some people do learn useful things from their first time around, but many embark upon new partnerships with the same ideal notions of parenting and marriage as they had before. If either of you have children, then there are extra challenges to be met this time as well as the usual adjustments of just getting used to living with someone.

Apart from the likelihood that our stereotype of the ideal family being made up of previously unmarried parents with two or three children may never have been realistic, there are nowadays some additional stresses which can cause relationships to end up being a disappointment. We tend to ask for very many different things from relationships, probably more than they can possibly provide. We hope to find the freedom to pursue our hopes and dreams and to grow and develop together, as well as individually, not limited by gender stereotypes; to enjoy sexual closeness that is mutually satisfying and to find stimulating companionship; and we even tend to rely on partnerships to provide personal strength and guidance that we might once have drawn from spiritual sources. All this at the same time as seeking status through work in our very achievement-oriented society, running a home, finding economic security, and raising children. The achievement of all these goals for each of the partners places a great deal of unfair pressure on relationships. When people's lives were more affected by basic things like finding food, health, surviving wars, natural fertility, traditional male/female duties and responsibilities, organised spirituality, and patriotism, than they are now (at least in Western affluent cultures), there was little room for partners to ask of their relationships the things many of us have now come to expect from them. There seemed to be a stronger sense of commitment to partner and family in the face of these influences.

Marriages are hardly ever really perfect, but perhaps too often we think they can be and are unwilling to settle for less. Marriages need to be workable partnerships where each person feels reinforced and supported by the other more often than they feel disappointed or undermined by them, and where there is open trusting communication.

When a relationship breaks down we usually find ourselves embarking on another one, often sooner rather than later, because we still have the same needs which we hoped our failed partnership would fulfil. And this time we have an additional set of demands to place on our next relationship – our children from the partnership we left behind. Their links with the past and our obligation to respect, sustain and encourage them are therefore an everyday part of modern parenting in more and more marriages.

Added to the extra demands of children from earlier partnerships are our own attitudes and feelings about our separation, which we often carry with us for some time. We need to be able to understand and accept them because they affect how we handle our new partnerships, as well as influencing our children's easy passage between their two parents.

Separation, recovery, new insights

Separating is really a process rather than an event. You both have to 'disengage' from your life together and it takes time to adjust to the emotions of it all. This is true for both of you in different ways at different times, however one-sided the decision to separate may have seemed at the time. When you look back on it all now maybe you can see that before you parted there was a long period when one of you felt there were problems. Maybe the other didn't want to recognise this and you couldn't discuss your feelings very productively. This often means that at the time you actually separated you weren't able to jointly prepare yourselves for it because your feelings about parting weren't the same. So it all probably happened in a less than ideal way for the children, because you were understandably preoccupied with your own position.

Recovering from a sense of failure, a lost love and a damaged self-image, and adjusting to a different way of life yourself affects how well you can help your children do their own adjusting. After all, you've got to meet with the source of your disappointment – your partner – to make a lot of decisions about the future, and while you're still trying to deal with your feelings about the failed marriage this isn't at all easy. Some people get stuck with hurt feelings and destructive attitudes for quite a time, and these 'divorce ghosts' have a way of reappearing, interfering with sensible communication between parents about their children. More on this in Chapter 3.

Time, effort, positive thinking and some constructive self-analysis will help you reorganise your relationship with your 'ex' so it's detached and cooperative. *Achieving a dignified detachment from the past and an acceptance of current circumstances is the most important step in getting on with your life so your children can get on with theirs.* Until you are able to do this (and for many people it takes some time), you'll find that your approach to life, your children and your 'ex' is affected by feelings, attitudes, actions and words which don't help at all. You'll find yourself wanting to pick fault, complain, resent, play 'tit-for-tat', cry 'poor me', wallow in guilt and self-pity, and many other feelings which don't make the children's position any easier, and which in happier and easier periods of your life you certainly wouldn't be very proud of.

However hard you may be trying to cover up your feelings for the children's sake, you may not succeed in concealing your sentiments entirely. Once you've truly resolved your feelings about your breakup you'll be able to leave behind these unhelpful feelings and attitudes, because you're feeling better about yourself and your life.

Old partnerships over time

As time goes on and you've pretty well detached yourself from the past, you'll find that your bond with your 'ex' weakens further despite your joint commitment to the children. You'll be inclined to communicate less as old links weaken and you fill your life with new people and new interests. You'll have started to take the past for granted, and the children will have too, to some degree. If something bugs you, you simply mightn't feel inclined to talk it over with this person you feel more and more estranged from because your lives have both moved onwards. But as the children grow and change, so do their needs, and issues will arise which affect the way their contact with both of you is managed, and which are still ideally best dealt with by you both. As the years go on, you'll find you're much more inclined to deal with issues on your own (with the help of your new partner) or through the children. Unless it's anything major, like a change of living arrangements, then this is usually fine and is more realistic for most people than getting together regularly to discuss the children.

There's another aspect of relationships over time which may affect how you feel about shared parenting. You'll find you both grow and change, sometimes in ways you won't feel sympathetic about. When you fall in love, a process of merging begins which makes you become a bit more like each other in your values, interests and lifestyles. You take an interest in, and often come to like, things you mightn't have experienced if you hadn't met this person. It's part of the joy of discovering people, extending your horizons through them. You also become more similar through giving up things you used to do before you met, because there's less time now or because the other doesn't particularly share your interest. Becoming more similar is a natural part of a close, life-sharing relationship. Having children together further contributes to the process. Once you separate, though, all these shared things that grew because of your close association are left behind. So the longer you're separated from your former partner the less like them you become. Rediscovering your self-image and sense of identity as an individual rather than as part of a couple is a normal and necessary part of adjusting to being separated. It involves a certain amount of experimenting in new areas, as well as deliberately freeing yourself from the ties and associations of the lost partnership. Once you meet someone new the process of becoming closer through sharing starts to operate all over again with the new and different person, and their own circle of friends and interests.

The point of describing all this is that you may find that as time goes on you feel more and more estranged from your children's other parent, feel increasingly on a different 'wavelength', and consequently mystified and frustrated, even though you've long since left behind any bitterness or sadness about your failed relationship. You've each gone your separate ways, taken on new ideas, made new friends, even adopted different lifestyles. This is a potential negative factor for shared parenting because it means that you may become even less compatible now you're separated than you were when together. This makes couple solidarity – essential to effective parenting – very difficult to sustain. You may find you disagree on more aspects of parenting as time goes on.

You have to allow people, including your 'ex', the freedom to change, to explore whatever directions they choose, however mistaken, misguided or transient they might seem to you, or however undesirable an influence you think they are on the children. It's important that you both understand the effects of new directions and new people on your children, and essential that you accept them or else they will contribute to misunderstanding and resentment. Fortunately, what you've learnt with time and experience about people, relationships and attitudes will help you realise that there isn't much useful influence you can have on a person you aren't involved with. They have the right to be the way they are, and your way of doing things (which you *can* influence and *are* responsible for) will be a significant part of your children's experience, and therefore available to be admired and accepted by them, by them because you are their parent. You *will* influence your children, though perhaps not obviously in the short term, even if you spend less time with them than your 'ex' does.

Always a parent

It's unlikely that you need any convincing about the worth of shared parenting after divorce, especially if you know that your children, because of their age and bonds with both of you, are going to go on needing you both and will obviously miss out if your divorce costs them a parent. So you probably don't even question it. Generally, it's obvious that it's going to be important that as much as possible of family life as they know it survives your separation.

But in certain circumstances it's not quite so obvious, and some people see it all quite differently because of their own unique circumstances:

Amy's baby daughter was only eighteen months when Greg decided he was going to leave. They'd been having problems for some time. Amy thought their relationship would survive her involvement with motherhood, which she acknowledged might have been making Greg feel left out. But, as it turned out, for Greg the problems went much deeper than this and when he left Amy was really hurt that he hadn't stayed around to try harder at working things out. She felt he had abandoned not only her but his baby daughter, and when he tried to set up some arrangements for seeing Katy, Amy found herself resenting his interest in the baby. After all, he hadn't paid much attention to her before, and surely it would be best to make a clean break and start again? She'd probably find a new father-figure for Katy in due course. Greg obviously didn't really care for Katy or he would have made more effort to save the marriage, and Katy wouldn't miss a father she had never really known. Unknown to Amy because of her own hurt and disappointment over breaking up, Greg had been struggling with feelings of guilt and uncertainty about what would happen to his potential relationship with Katy if he left. He was also aware of the difficulties he'd had in contributing as a parent so far because of his difficulties with Amy. He was determined not to relinquish his responsibilities for Katy just because he couldn't work things out with Amy.

This story isn't an unusual one. There's somehow an extra sense of sadness about having to separate when a child is very young, even though from the child's point of view it's often easier. It's as if family and friends are somehow thinking, 'How could they have gone ahead with becoming parents if they knew they had problems?' But of course human relationships and emotions are not logical or planned or well understood. People's feelings and reactions about this kind of separation set the scene for mothers (and sometimes their friends and relations too), to question whether a relationship with an absent parent is worth cultivating. It's difficult for them to separate their own feelings about the deservingness of the 'deserting' parent from the child's long-term needs, or to appreciate the potential contribution the departed parent has to offer their child.

Some fathers, especially when faced with this kind of attitude on the part of their child's mother, decide (and it must sometimes be a very hard decision to make) not to even attempt to have an active parenting role and opt out of their child's life entirely. There are of course circumstances when this is a realistic and wise decision which does no appreciable harm, so long as the child isn't misled about their origins.

Other parents start off spending time fairly regularly with their children after separating, but as time goes on, and everyone's circumstances change, their contact becomes less and less frequent and may stop altogether. For many children this may be a considerable loss. Biological origins are important to people's sense of identity; and biological links can't, like marriages, be replaced or undone.

What the research says

Although most readers won't need persuading, here's what the experts have to say about the needs of children of divorce – for those who want more insight into what they're already committed to, for those who find it a struggle sometimes, and for those who aren't so certain that it's worth it.

Not so long ago it used to be thought that children from what were called 'broken homes' were by definition off to a bad start in life and were definitely traumatised by their parents' separation. But as marriage breakdown became more common, providing an incentive for more good-quality research to be done, this viewpoint changed. It became obvious that the extent to which children are affected by divorce depends on how much conflict they are exposed to during the marriage and after the separation. Clearly, in many families a separation brings a welcome improvement in the child's family circumstances through relief from conflict. So it isn't the fact of a divorce, but rather the family circumstances both before and after the separation that have the effect. Continuing family conflict is known to be psychologically damaging to children, rather than the event of divorce itself. Not such a remarkable finding really, but reassuring!

Researchers also have shown that the happiest children of divorce are those who are supported and sustained through the years after their parents' separation by being able to enjoy free-and-easy continuous relationships with both their parents.

For years after a separation and right into adulthood, children go on wishing that their parents had stayed together. Even children who remember experiencing a lot of conflict at home would rather their parents hadn't split up.

These findings mean therefore that since your children would probably much rather you stuck together, you should try hard to improve your relationship. But if you can't get your marriage to work and you must separate, then successful cooperative parenting after divorce is the most valuable thing you can give your children to compensate for not having been able to go on living together. This makes obvious sense, but again it's reassuring to know that the research supports us.

Why it's worth it

You're probably a long way from inflicting serious levels of conflict on your children, but you may feel that sharing an important responsibility with someone you don't care for or feel interested in any more is a burden sometimes. When you wonder if the whole business of shared parenting from two different camps is all worth it, with the ongoing compromises, exasperations and timetabling of it all, you can reassure yourself by recalling the many reasons why it is worth it, and why it's so important to get it right:

- Getting a system going promptly so that the children spend time with the parent who moved out helps them with thoughts like 'if I had behaved myself better and not caused so many arguments between them, he wouldn't have gone, so it must be my fault; if he could hurt my feelings so much by going, he mustn't love me any more'. It's not at all uncommon for children to blame themselves for their parents' separation, especially if they recall parental tensions being focused, as they often are, on issues to do with them.

- Children can feel rejected and abandoned by the parent who moves elsewhere, however mutual the decision to separate was. Contact with the parent who 'leaves' helps reassure them that this bond is not altered, it just has to be reorganised, and protects against damage to their self-esteem and emerging sense of identity.

- Children have a tendency to fill gaps in their knowledge and thinking with fantasy. Regular contact with a part-time parent enables them to sustain a concept of that parent based on reality, rather than what they want to believe, or feel pressured to believe because of one parent's feelings about the other.

- Children who feel they have 'lost' a parent because they 'went away' may worry about the remaining parent leaving too. This can mean that their sense of security is threatened so they are likely to incorporate the attitudes and feelings of their major caretaker, sometimes at the expense of their relationship with the part-time parent. They align themselves with the remaining parent to safeguard this relationship. There's more on this in Chapter 8. Continuing contact with both parents helps restore a sense of security about the family and enables them to have relationships with each that are more independent.

- Today's shared parenting, with both fathers and mothers contributing substantially (and often other caretakers too), has shown that children can have significant bonds with many people from a very early age. Families make us feel a sense of love and obligation towards both our parents, so children can really pine for relationships lost through separation even though the love of their major caretaker remains constant. And their self-esteem and emerging sense of identity may be affected in significant ways.

In a nutshell then, divorce itself isn't damaging, but if you're not emotionally detached and flexible, you may be contributing to the fact that your child's post-divorce life is. Actively encouraging a positive relationship between your children and both their parents is the best thing you can give them to make up for being divorced. They can't have this without *both* of you contributing in useful ways.

Cultivating helpful attitudes

To help achieve positive relationships all round here's how you should start:

• Realise that there's always more than one point of view on things, and that for any relationship to work, each person must allow the other room to have their own opinions and feelings about things, and respect their position without necessarily agreeing with it. Never make a person feel you dismiss their point of view. Everyone wants to feel they're listened to. You might think that you always do, but check from time to time that however good your intentions are, your partner really feels you do listen. You'll find all your differences of opinion with your former partner harder to deal with now because they're no longer able to be balanced out with love like in the good old days, and because all the differences are now centred on the children, for whom your love hasn't changed. Remember, they have two parents who are different people with different strengths and weaknesses, both of whom in their own individual ways are important sources of learning for them. When you get exasperated, try to see it this way, and always be prepared not only to listen, but also to compromise.

• Recognise that it's difficult to have real solidarity as a couple when you don't see or talk to each other much. But this is what children need in a family. Aim to be a team in regard to your children. It *is* possible to be reasonably united about them on minimum communication, especially if you can be detached enough from issues of fairness, deservingness and blame, to see that making compromises rather than pressing a point just for the sake of it is often worthwhile.

When my wife moved house we had to reorganise my time with the children because it was a two-hour drive away. Sadly, it meant me seeing them less often because of the travel, and fortnightly weekends were the only feasible possibility. I thought they could come to me on a Friday afternoon and I offered to collect them. My logic was that to come that distance they might as well come for as long a weekend as they could. I'd make sure they were home at a reasonable hour on a Sunday afternoon. But Jenny reckoned that this wouldn't suit, it would have to be from Saturday morning or they'd be too tired, there'd be homework to be done, they'd arrive after dark in winter and various other reasons. I really felt she was being inflexible and not considering my point of view. After all, it wasn't me who'd moved away, and I knew the boys enjoyed their time with me, and they could bring their homework with them. But she wouldn't agree to Fridays, and I ended up having to accept what she would allow, because to do anything else would have stirred up a lot of ill-feeling. It didn't seem fair and it was hard trying to convince myself that her point of view might seem logical and reasonable to her. I'm hoping that after they get used to their new surroundings and the travelling, we'll be able to renegotiate about Friday evenings.

- At the helm of your new family, it's even more important than before to have couple solidarity because you have the extra challenges of 'step-relationships'. You can't effectively manage all the complex relationships (and families *are* complex) and meet everyone's changing needs, without the authority of united leadership. Make sure you set aside time to talk over family policies and practices regularly as a couple and include time to share your feelings trustingly about everyone – the good ones as well as the bad ones!

- Make a personal resolution with yourself to communicate your feelings as honestly as you can, provided there's a useful purpose to it, without being destructive. Then people close and therefore important to you can take into account your needs and feelings and respect your individuality and your opinions, because you are genuine. People cannot respect your point of view or take it into account if you don't communicate it, and communicate it accurately.

- When you feel needy, a bit hard done by, or just lonely, do a double check on yourself to make sure you aren't drawing more emotional support from your children than is really good for them. Being a parent after a separation can be more lonely than you expected and you'll feel inadequate at times. Financial hardship is often a real drain too. The children need you to be involved, enthusiastic, reliable and consistent, which will seem a tall order when you're feeling low. They don't need to see you as down and fragile to the extent that they have to worry about you, or feel they have to provide you with sympathy, support and companionship at the expense of their own such needs. But obviously you can't always cover up or deny your feelings. Try to be real and human rather than controlled and edgy, so the children feel able to open up to you when they want to, but don't feel they have to worry about how you are. You can acknowledge some of your feelings to them if you take care to do it in a way that doesn't make you seem frail as a parent, as if you need them.

They need to see you strong and positive about the future, so their own sense of security about it is preserved.

To begin with I thought I absolutely mustn't show my true feelings of hopelessness, rage and disappointment to the children (two boys aged nine and eleven), that they must be protected from the emotions of our marriage at all costs. But after a while I realised that not only was this pretty impossible, but that I wasn't being genuine with them and this was starting to spoil our communication. We certainly didn't need any more problems! So I started talking to them a bit about what I was going through emotionally, being careful not to make them think my sadness or irritability was their father's fault, but just a part of life. I tried to show them what helped me keep going, and that acknowledging your feelings helps. If I got short with one of them unreasonably, as soon as I realised I'd done it, I'd give him a big cuddle and say something like, 'Sorry I sounded so cross about that, it wasn't fair on you. I was feeling cranky and I took it out on you by mistake. What you did wasn't really all that naughty, but sometimes people do overreact. Silly of me, wasn't it?' Then I'd change the subject. I hope I pitched it right so they felt I was in charge of my feelings and not all over the place and unpredictable. It certainly made it easier for us to feel positive most of the time and to keep up the humour and lightheartedness. Learning to laugh at yourself helps. And I kept my really powerful emotional sessions till I could be with a sympathetic friend!

• If you're still a bit preoccupied with who did what and said what in the past and who believes whose version of it all, you may find yourself anxious that the children see you as you think they should. It's hard when they come up with their own questions about the past, and you must answer in a constructive but not in a finger-pointing way. You may be tempted to involve them in your adult emotional business because you're worried about what they may be thinking about you, or about the influence of the other parent on their thoughts about these grown-up matters. It's harder still if you feel concerned about how their relationship with a step-parent (your 'ex's' new partner) is going to develop. It's natural, but not usually necessary, to fear being 'replaced' by an alternative same-sex parent. If you do get into a detailed discussion about family events and personalities you may place children in a conflict of loyalties that can be emotionally quite cruel. Realise that separated parents are often worried about how much influence they will respectively have on their children as time goes on. Understandably they have doubts about how much of a useful parent they will really be able to be. Try to believe in yourself and what you can offer the children without feeling the need to prove it to them by setting the record straight or asserting your biological superiority over a step-parent.

- There's often something else at work within this uncertainty about the strength of your bonds with your child. It's an aspect of the loyalty triangle which children have to come to grips with. They want and need to go on loving two people who don't love each other. Since you no longer love their other parent and aren't part of your children's relationship with this person any more, there may be a subtle sense of having become rivals for your children's affections. They may now seem in your mind to have a choice about where to place their loyalties, a choice they didn't really have when you all lived together. You may find yourself worrying about how much time they want to spend with you, about whether it's more fun for them at Dad's place, or is their bond with Mum growing stronger at the expense of their ties and loyalties towards you? If you are feeling lonely, isolated from your family, or you haven't really got your life reorganised yet, these sorts of doubts may affect the way you relate to your children so that you're not giving them the freedom they should have to adjust to and enjoy their new relationships. It will be affected by various obligations, demands and pressures, because of where they sense you're at. You're leaning on them a bit too much because of your own needs and a new sense of competing parental influences. You need to acquire the personal strength not to be threatened by or jealous of your child having strong emotional links with someone who is now outside your family circle, a relationship of which you can't be a part. This can take some adjusting to and requires a sense of personal security that is often shaken after a separation.

- Never lose sight of the fact that your children are entitled to enjoy the freedom to relate to both their parents (and step-parents too) in their own way, at their own pace, taking in and making some sort of sense of the various personalities of everyone concerned. You can't expect to be able to influence how your children react to their other parent or to a step-parent, how much of their characteristics and standards they choose to model, internalise or ignore. 'Letting go' of your children and passing gracefully from the period when your children are completely dependent on you and you directly share all of their waking experience, to allowing them to have separate experiences you are not at all part of, is a milestone every parent, especially mothers, must pass. It can be much harder to do this when your children are spending impressionable time with someone you have emotional feeling for, whether this person is your children's natural parent or a step-parent.

Here are the helpful attitudes to cultivate, in a summary checklist:

1. Listen, and leave room for other points of view.
2. Be a team as parents, willing to compromise sometimes.
3. Use your primary relationship to support each other, consult and plan for the family.
4. Communicate your own views and feelings authentically.

5. Be emotionally strong for the children.
6. Don't try to prove your worth to the children by going over events in the family's history.
7. Don't let yourself need the children too much.
8. Allow them emotional freedom.

3

Successful Team Parenting from Different Camps

This really begins at the time when you decided you were going to separate. It's at this point that the basis of your parenting had to change, with undertakings being made about how you were going to reorganise your relationship as parents because of living separately. Hopefully you were able to do this together, because cooperative discussion about the things that are happening in a relationship and what the future holds (in other words, taking responsibility for the partnership rather than running away from it) is the beginning of effective parenting after separation.

Planning your children's two-household family

Your two-household family will get off to a good start if you can tell your children together about your decision to separate and give them a bit of an explanation about why it has to happen and how the future will work out. Naturally in the midst of all the sadness about your marriage, you mightn't be able to meet this ideal, but at least try to agree on when you're going to talk to them and what you're each going to say. They need to feel you're still going to be a team about them, making plans together and looking after their interests. If you can't announce your decision together because one of you has already left, or you know it will be unpleasantly emotional and therefore unmanageable to try and do it as a family, then you have to do it on your own and give as much reassurance about the

43

future as you can. Hopefully you'll be able to tell them where everyone will be living and how they'll be seeing both of you regularly.

If you manage to talk to the children together despite the sadness of the event, congratulations. What you decide for them will probably work well, and if it doesn't you'll no doubt be able to meet up to do some fine tuning together.

WHERE SHOULD IT HAPPEN?

As soon as possible, Dad (or Mum if she's to be the 'visited' parent) should set up some sort of home base. Using the family home is usually a strain for everyone and conducting an intimate relationship in zoos and cafes can be expensive, tiring and not very realistic. The children will need to reassure themselves about your surroundings, which very much govern whether you are alright in their minds. Don't worry about whether your accommodation is all that adequate for the time being, as children love camping out on floors and are usually much more flexible than adults about territory and privacy. If you're really stuck because you haven't organised yourself yet, use a friend's or relation's place. But you should aim for having some territory in your home that's identifiably theirs.

HOW LONG FOR?

There's no real reason why children shouldn't see as much of Dad as is feasible. But it's often hard to find time to fit everything in and some activities may have to be given up to allow enough parenting time. Many children miss their 'lost' parent, and for young children a fortnight is a long time. Telephone contact can be a reassuring link between households. The further apart you live, the longer the visits may need to be, so that no one has to spend too much of the agreed time travelling.

HOW OFTEN?

How regular the visits are rather than how often or for how long they last is usually more important for the children in the long term. They like to know when they are next going to see Dad and leaving it open may seem uncertain and uncommitted. Knowing when gives them a sense of continuity. If you really don't know when it can be, make a reassuring promise about when you're going to let them know, making sure you keep Mum informed. Even if you're the easy-going type and advance planning isn't really your style, try to make a special effort for a while – your children may be feeling a bit uncertain about how it's all going to work out and worried about losing you.

Infants and very young children often fare best with shorter and more frequent visits away from Mum, but of course this'll depend on whether they have older brothers and sisters and whether they're used to being with alternative caretakers. Very young children may not like being separated from their mother, and some infants go through quite normal periods of clinging to their familiar person when separation is imminent. The visited parent – usually Dad – should perhaps arrange to be with them at home for a while on a few closely consecutive occasions before taking them out to somewhere familiar without their Mum. With the right handling (and this includes close consultation with Mum), most children soon get used to separations from their main caretaker, though some take longer than others to pass this milestone. Children are growing and developing all the time of course, and rapidly in their first few years of life. Arrangements will need to be adjusted often to suit their changing needs.

If you do live far apart, don't despair. It is possible for important bonds to grow and develop when there are quite long gaps between contact, especially if everyone makes an effort to sustain links between visits in positive ways, with letters, calls, tapes etc. They may miss Dad a lot between times though, and you may find it's worth compromising an ideal in order to stay closer and have more frequent contact.

TIMETABLING THE VISITS

There isn't any special formula for the right timetable for visiting. The best arrangements are those which you can work out yourselves, taking into account the children's ages, personalities and needs, as well as the commitments and responsibilities of you two parents (and often step-parents, too). You are obviously in the best position to know what's going to suit everyone involved, in a manageable and positive way. The children will settle into their new divided situation most easily if they feel they can have free and easy contact with both of you, without there being any problem about it. It should be taken for granted as 'normal'. Often this ideal is easiest if you live close to each other and the children can cycle or walk to and fro between their homes and have a key to both. Weekday access often isn't possible because of distance, but there's no reason not to include it if you want to. You are the best judge of your child's fatigue levels and the extent of their other after-school commitments.

If you have more than one child, it's usually best that they have their time with each parent all together, especially to begin with. They can be of enormous comfort and support to each other, and any insecurities, jealousies and imagined favouritism will be minimised if they all visit Dad together. Use your common sense about this though, because if they have wide-ranging ages and interests then obviously some dovetailing of the arrangements and taking turns is going to be sensible.

Although there's nothing really tried and tested about the fortnightly weekend arrangement that a lot of families seem to have, it suits many people with younger school-aged children, at least during term-time, because:

- It's often easier for one parent to be responsible for everything associated with the usual weekday routine, whether or not they work outside as well as inside the home.
- Many fathers (and mothers for that matter) aren't in a position to spend much time with their children during the week. Many women are already geared up to running a home, being a parent and going out to work and it suits the family in most respects for this arrangement to continue.
- If much travel is involved, weekends are the only practical possibility, and overnight stays can be enjoyed, giving Mum a break and Dad a chance for some real family experience.
- Alternate weekends leave Mum some day leisure time with the children and allow for social and recreational activities associated with their usual community.

It's very good if the children can spend some school holiday time with their 'part-time' parent. It makes for a more relaxed experience all round than is possible with the somewhat hurried routine of weekends, and enables important bonds to develop further. Many parents think that half of all school holidays is reasonable, but of course it all very much depends on both parents' lifestyle, work commitments and new family circumstances. There's no point in deciding on half the school holidays each just because it seems fair, if it's not feasible for one or both of you. For more on having your children stay with you in school holidays, see Chapter 4.

You'll realise by now that a lot of the planning points we've mentioned so far are really what your common sense would tell you if you'd let it guide you. So use it, and don't get too earnest and rigid about the whole thing! Be respectfully flexible.

Making it work

Once you've got some sort of a plan and it's under way, you'll need to keep an eye on how everything's going so you're one step ahead of any possible problems, and don't miss out on opportunities to improve things. Remember, this two-way parenting lasts till the children are grown up, so keep an eye on what you're both doing:

- Try to tell each other things about the children's needs and preferences and habits, just as you would tell anybody else the children were visiting without you. Dad is sure to be out of touch with their everyday experiences, joys and interests. Keep each other informed about things that concern the children. Think of this as an essential principle of good team-management and communication rather than as telling each other how to look after the children properly!

- Try to keep punctual to avoid misunderstandings, without being too rigid about necessary alterations. Flexibility is fine if you're communicating about it reasonably together.

- Be encouraging about the visits so the children really feel you want them to have a good time, aren't going to be too lonely without them, or do too many exciting-sounding things while they're gone!

- If you wonder how good he is with the children, try to give him the benefit of the doubt. Sometimes it's hard to be trusting when you feel you're carrying most of the responsibility for the children on your own and you don't remember him being much of a father before you separated. People's motivation often changes in surprising ways after a life change. Many fathers rediscover the enjoyment of their children and an appreciation of parenting responsibilities only when they're away from an unsatisfactory marriage. This happened to Doug in Chapter 1. It's a good thing.

- Don't forget obvious courtesies like sending the children with suitable clothing, returning clothes and belongings, and being ready for pickups and returns. If they want very much to take something to Dad's that will cause a nuisance if it gets left there, be sure to tell Dad so it's less likely to be forgotten.

- Try not to be too particular about the children's clothes and belongings getting left behind or coming back in a mess or damaged. There are bound to be some accidents and omissions which might seem annoying, but making an issue of it doesn't often achieve much and may just make the children think their visits to Dad are a nuisance to you. Include a list of clothes and belongings you send with them, to help him return them all when they come home to you. Stick to giving him the occasional gentle reminder. Older children can of course take more responsibility for their belongings. Dad can help things run smoothly in this department too (see Chapter 4).
- Have a fixed timetable for visits and stick to it so that everyone knows what's happening. Then the children aren't disappointed, and neither of you is inconvenienced unnecessarily. Flexibility is possible and desirable if it's not exploited, but a timetable which you may vary if necessary is usually best all round, so you don't have to keep on contacting each other before arranging anything.
- If you sometimes feel it's a grind to manage all the organising, timetabling and discussion that's involved, try to adjust your thinking so you look upon this 'post-divorce parenting' as a challenge in which you can excel.
- Remind yourself of how important it all is for your children in the long term and this will help.
- Remember, it's not easy being a part-time parent either. From his point of view, the limitations of only being able to have occasional contact with his own children can be very frustrating and sad.
- Don't judge your partner's competence as a parent by how you saw them during the marriage. Take what the children come home telling you with a pinch of salt, but listen to it. There isn't much you can do about it unless you really do get on well with your 'ex', and anyway there's always room for more than one way of doing things.

49

- Fathers who have had little to do with their young children won't turn into skilled parents overnight, and can use the help of friends and relations. Don't be tempted to see his involving others as him not making proper use of his time with the children. They'll benefit from contact with his friends and relations as long as they also have plenty of time with him.

- Don't give the children too much choice about the arrangements. Although children often resist direction, they'll appreciate the clear commitment to their visits that you show if you encourage them to go with confidence, certainty and enthusiasm (no matter what you yourself feel at times about their Dad!).

- Children don't like being quizzed about what's going on in their 'other home' or being made to carry messages between you. They'll tell you what they want you to know. Avoid using your children as 'go-betweens' because you can't talk to each other. It can cause all sorts of misunderstandings and tensions, especially when they get messages about arrangements or instructions wrong.

- Part-time parenting is different from everyday contact with your children and is sometimes hard to adjust to. Dad often feels cut off from the children, and finds himself giving them more treats than Mum approves of. A bit of acceptance and appreciation of your respective different kinds of contact with the children will go a long way towards preventing unnecessary resentment.

- Try to be flexible about Christmas, birthdays and other special days. Children don't mind events not being celebrated on the correct day unless they know you do.

- Try to be accepting of new partnerships that are bound to develop for both of you, and which will involve the children. It's sometimes worth postponing the introduction of new people while visiting patterns are getting established. After all, time with a parent is the most important, and children as well as adults can be a bit sensitive about new liaisons. There's more on this in Chapters 4 and 5.

When it's hard to talk to each other

At times when communication isn't all that good between you, although you know you're both trying not to let old feelings for one another interfere, you're sometimes going to get exasperated and need some extra insight, patience and sensitivity. This will either be because you haven't been separated for all that long and you're both still feeling mistrustful, or because some 'old wounds' have opened up, which sometimes happens when a major family event takes place like remarriage or moving house. Don't give up on trying to communicate with each other about the children. Being able to talk without 'hanging up' is crucial, and it will get better, especially if you're willing to compromise a bit.

You might be surprised at how, just when you thought you 'had it all together' about the past, irritations can resurface. The reappearance of 'divorce ghosts' (see also Chapter 2) is just a reminder of the reasons why you couldn't live together. Take a deep breath, remind yourself that you don't *have* to let your 'ex' get to you, and check with yourself or with a friend whether whatever it is *really matters*! Put aside your exasperation about him, realise the fruitlessness of wanting things to be fair, of blaming yourself, your 'ex' or anybody else, and tackle life positively for the children's benefit, as well as for the sake of your own dignity and good humour.

Some common concerns

If the children occasionally show reluctance to go from one home to the other, be prepared to use some fairly firm but supportive persuasion. This'll probably only happen in the early months of your new arrangements while they're getting used to it, unless something else is on their minds. It's unlikely that there'd be anything worrying them about the visits themselves other than apprehension about a handover or return. A common reason for children being uncertain about visiting Dad, to the point where they say they don't want to go, is doubt about whether both parents really approve of the continuing contact. For the sake of your children's position, you both need to be positive and enthusiastic about each other. This especially applies to Mum when encouraging children to get ready to go and see Dad. Reassuring them that you more than approve, you enthuse, will help a lot.

With young children, it's often not so much that they don't want to do what they have to do, but that they're absorbed in what's happening now with you, not what's in store for later. Don't make the mistake of mentioning the forthcoming visit too often or too far in advance, as this has a way of conveying your worry about how they're going to handle it (and how you're going to handle him!), which will make *them* apprehensive. Discuss it a day or so beforehand, so they can think about it, what they might take and what they might tell him about, etc. Even if you both handle the handover well, it can still be a time that is a bit upsetting simply because it is such a clear reminder that Mum and Dad don't live together any more and that their two worlds really are separate. This is a sad fact for children and always will be. But life contains many sad facts which can't be changed, so give them the same comfort and understanding you would give them about anything else, without making too much of it.

Sporting and social engagements at weekends are sometimes another problem, and you need to get together to sort out your children's priorities for them. Don't worry if they show some resistance to what you've agreed on for them, try to be firm.

Older children, especially ones who are getting used to the situation, may find routine scheduled visits unattractive because they don't seem interesting enough or because they want to be busy with their own affairs. Dad obviously has to find a way of life which allows interesting activities and flexibility during visits, and timing may have to be altered to suit the children more too. Mum must do better than say 'Well, you don't have to go out with him if you don't want to' or 'Please yourself', just because they're allowed to please themselves over a lot of other things. It's often a mistake to give older children too much freedom of choice, although obviously some parents don't get very far trying to force teenagers to do things they don't want to! Once they're out of touch with a parent, whatever the reason, it'll be far more difficult for children to re-establish a relationship which is important to them.

You needn't feel that children will necessarily be confused by being part of two families where the rules, activities and lifestyles are different. The two of you as parents will develop new ways of doing things and new priorities now you're apart, especially if you have found new partners (see Chapter 2). Children can adapt provided the rules in each place are clear and consistent, and provided the differences are respected and not made too much of by either of you. It can be enriching to grow up experiencing more than one way of living in the sense that it can provide children with the opportunity to learn open-mindedness, respect and flexibility, as well as have wider-ranging experiences than they would otherwise.

At first I was pretty horrified at the way the children's table manners seemed to be heading, but felt I couldn't keep going on about it because it seemed to sound as if I was criticising them personally and their mother for what she had (or, in this case hadn't) taught them. And how could they be expected to cope with different ways in different households? We'd surely given them enough to have to adjust to as it was. And they seemed fussy about what they ate, always seeming to want things that I didn't consider good for them. But as time went on mealtimes stopped being the pleasant occasions that I wanted them to be, and my wife found it all very hard. We talked about it for ages together and finally decided that since in most other respects our time with my children was very relaxed and pleasant, that the time had come to stop worrying about the children getting confused by having to adapt to two standards, or about them feeling criticised, and we introduced a new policy about mealtimes. We just explained it in terms of our expectations and wishes about what we wanted in this household. When they piped up with, 'Dad, why do we have to stay sitting till everyone's finished?' we just said we thought what Mum allowed was fine, but here we like to do things a bit differently. And we stuck to our usual menu more often instead of listening to what they thought they wanted all the time. Within a couple of weekends mealtimes had improved a lot and I really don't think confusion is the issue for them that I thought it was.

Children benefit by feeling the security of decisions about their lives being made for them. You probably know this and put it into practice over issues you feel certain about, like whether they should go to school or watch a certain TV programme, but when you're a bit worried about what's best for them (or you're a bit apprehensive about the whole shared parenting business), then it's not so easy to give clear and hence respected directions to the children. It is important to avoid giving them too much choice about their visiting arrangements. Best of all, have them know that decisions are being made by both of you about them, despite your differences which should be kept as separate adult business. The trick is, as with a lot of parenting policies that have to be devised, to make the children feel they've had a say, expressed what they think are their preferences, been listened to, but that you, as parent, have made the decision and take responsibility for it. This aspect of effective communication comes up again in Chapter 7. Once they are in their teens they can start to have a say and can begin to make their own arrangements with Dad in consultation with you.

Financial matters sometimes become a sore point. Money, the having and the not having of it, tends to pervade people's thinking probably more than we might realise or care to admit! It may be tempting to think Dad doesn't deserve to see the children if he doesn't pay you the amount for their upkeep he agreed to, or that you think he could and should pay. This is understandably infuriating but at all costs try to keep money matters out of the children's awareness. They shouldn't be made to feel that their relationship with a missed and loved parent depends on the payment of money. Fathers may not always feel sympathetic about their 'ex' not earning an income when this means they have to pick up the tab themselves. But your differences of opinion about money, property and possessions are part of your relationship difficulties and are nothing to do with the children, even though they are affected by them. Watch how much you involve them in discussions about what you can and can't afford and why, because it's bound to create confusion, doubt and hurt in the children's minds, which they can do without. Be strong, authoritative and reassuring in answer to their questions about money so they don't feel they have to concern themselves about which parent's doing the right thing, and so they do feel you are able to work these things out together, rather than at loggerheads.

Fielding children's questions well

Try to allow your children the opportunity to communicate their feelings about their family situation without expecting them to understand or articulate them very well, and certainly without pressing them. It's quite difficult for children to understand how it is possible to go on loving two people who no longer love each other. It seems like an impossible triangle. We've mentioned that as time goes on children go on wanting their parents to get back together, and start asking themselves and you more questions about why things are the way they are. Try to answer their questions without undermining their feelings about the other parent's worth, even if a little withholding of the truth (as you see it) is involved.

They don't have to know the truth about who's to blame or who did what in the past, even though you may very much want them to know and accept your version of events, because you know it's the right one. We showed how you need to cultivate a helpful attitude about this in Chapter 2. When they ask questions about the past, remember that much of what happens in adult relationships is far too complex for children to understand anyway (it's hard enough for adults a lot of the time!), and you may confuse them or misguide their loyalties. Try to convey your reasons for separating in a simple way with enough detail to satisfy their curiosity and make them feel it's not a taboo subject. A fairly general statement about parents liking each other in some ways but being unable to live together because you're too different on too many issues, will often be sufficient. Older children may start to want to know more, so try and make your discussion into something that may be useful to them as they learn about relationships for themselves.

It can be tricky answering children's questions when the honest answer would be a criticism of their other parent, especially if you're still a bit sore about it yourself. A lot of parents struggle over this issue of truth and what to say, as Adrian's Dad does in Chapter 9. Try not to lay blame on your 'ex' even if you think it's deserved. It will obviously be much harder for the children to go on loving you both freely if one is portrayed as having done great wrong to the other. And younger children tend to be rather black and white in their thinking. For example, if they think Dad has left for a new relationship, then he must be wicked through and through. Both of you need to help your children understand that their parents have many strengths and that these aren't cancelled out by faults.

Imaginary problems

One of the biggest dangers involved in sharing your children after a divorce is in reading too much into things your children do or say and accidentally creating problems that aren't really there. There are two reasons why this happens. First of all, you naturally want to do your utmost to help your children get over the sadness of their parents' separation and cope with the consequences. And if you're feeling guilty about what you've inflicted upon them you'll be really on the lookout for any difficulties they may be having. This can make you attribute too much significance to chance statements. So can your own leftover hurt feelings, which sometimes make you a bit too ready to criticise or blame your 'ex' on the basis of something you've heard from the children. (Step-parents often have a similar tendency to see things that may not be there, because of their own doubts about whether their step-children are accepting them – see Chapter 6).

We'd only been separated for about three months and I was particularly concerned as to how our thirteen-year-old was reacting to it all. He got me really worried one night when he said he didn't want me to come and watch his rowing regatta at the weekend. He wouldn't say why, just that he didn't want me there, and I'd always taken an interest in his sport and we get on pretty well together, so it took me by surprise. I thought, oh dear, it must be because his mother is planning to be there and he thinks it's going to be upsetting or embarrassing if we both go; and he's finding it too difficult to tell me this for fear of worrying me. How was I to handle this, I wondered? If I didn't go, he might feel I wasn't insistent or interested enough, even though he doesn't seem to want me there (is he testing out my continued interest in him, I wondered?). If I do go, it could be an important way of showing that we still both care and that it needn't be awkward for him. Or maybe he really doesn't want anything to do with either of his parents at the moment. Things were at a bit of a deadlock between myself and his mother and I couldn't talk to her about our son at all at this time. She just wasn't talking to me. Anyway, after thinking about it for ages and doing nothing for 24 hours, I decided to ask John whether he didn't want me there because his Mum was going. Imagine how silly I felt (and relieved too) when he said, quite cheerily, 'Oh no Dad, it's nothing like that, I've asked Mum not to be there either because I know I can row better than I am doing at the moment and I don't want either of you to watch me until I'm doing my best.' I needn't have worried at all!

Children are naturally pretty resilient, and may be managing better than you think they are. They also quite skilful in a mischievous way at manipulating their parents when their time with them is separate, and may be deliberately playing on your good intentions in order to gain some advantage. So before you decide there's a problem, 'stand back' and look at it as objectively as you can. If you still think there might be a problem, then get in touch with your 'ex' to discuss it.

Are we getting there?

If it all gets too much sometimes, you may wonder whether you're getting it as right as you should be. Or perhaps you feel either that he has all the fun and none of the responsibilities, or that she has all the intimacy and communication with them and they feel like little strangers to me. Refer back to the discussion in Chapter 2 on why it's worth it and remind yourself of a few facts:

- Continuing a relationship with both parents is probably the most important emotional support there is for children of divorce, if this is maintained and kept positive by both of them. This is so even when step-parents are involved.
- Visits help children not to blame themselves for their parents having separated, and help them not to feel rejected and discarded by the parent they can no longer see so often.

- Your point of view and your 'ex's' are bound to be different or you wouldn't have separated, so don't expect to be able to see eye-to-eye always on things to do with the children. Try to make your 'ex' feel you've really listened to his or her point of view.

- Once both of you have got over the breakup of your relationship and are getting on with your new lives, you'll find that you can be more flexible and easy-going about how you manage the children, because communication has improved. Being able to make a few compromises from time to time and not overly concerning yourself with fairness, blame and deservingness, will certainly help it all run smoothly, particularly during the sometimes delicate twelve-month period after a separation.

If you can be positive and consistent in the way you look after your children, whether you're on your own or have a new partner, you'll help give them the confidence to benefit from the reorganisation of their original family.

Summary

Here's a reminder of the main points of this chapter:

1. Keeping conflict between you and your 'ex' to a minimum is more important than anything else for the success of shared parenting. You must be able to talk to each other cordially, even if it's only on the doorstep or on the phone.

2. Regular contact with whichever of you is the 'part-time' parent is important, more important than the frequency and duration of the visits, to give your children a sense of continuity and security about both of you.

3. For your children to feel confident about visits, and to allow for essential flexibility and cooperation about fine tuning the

arrangements to suit everyone's changing needs and circumstances, there must be mutual respect and trust between you.

4. Watch out that you're not making your children feel they have too much say in the arrangements, especially to begin with, and remember you can unwittingly convey the idea that there's choice in rather subtle ways. Look forward to letting them make the decisions in future years, long after everyone's got used to easygoing and trusting movement between households.

5. Remember, *you* contribute to the way things are, so be prepared to look at yourself, take charge and even laugh at yourself. And aim for having fun in your family!

4

Making the Most of
Part-time Parenting

'Weekend', 'part-time', 'holiday' or 'occasional' parents (most often
fathers) get a chapter of their very own with good reason. Being an
effective parent when a large part of your child's daily experience
happens somewhere else, and is mostly only known to you if they
care to tell you about it, is quite a challenge. When you're getting
started with it, soon after your separation, it can be a rather uneasy
sort of role until you (and they) get used to it. And different issues
will arise as your children grow older and your own family
circumstances change.

In the beginning

To begin with you're sure to find yourself uncertain about how to
'be' with them, perhaps because you've never spent much time with
them on your own. Suddenly you discover that being solely
responsible for them for hours on end is very taxing, especially if
they're quite young. Constantly in the back of your mind is
uncertainty about how they're reacting to your being separated,
whether they're blaming you for breaking up the family, how you
can make their time with you interesting enough that they'll want
to come next time, whether if you discipline them too firmly they'll
reject you, and lots of other little concerns and doubts.

On top of all this you're having to deal with your own feelings
of isolation from the family. After all, you only left her, not your

children, didn't you? Worse still is the loneliness of getting used to feeling you've lost everything because she left with the children – you still love them all in spite of the difficulties you know you had, and dearly want everyone back together again. However much you know separating was the right decision, you probably aren't able to honestly say you have absolutely no regrets. Most fathers, in facing up to separating, don't want to have to lose touch with their children as well as with their mate. But they often feel that this is exactly what they've done – the price for changing partners is losing the whole family. This is a harsh but unchangeable fact about separations. Perhaps you've passed this early stage of adjusting to sharing the children in a new sort of way, and have a reasonably good to and fro arrangement going. To keep it working well though, it's going to need some fine tuning. Parenting is challenging at the best of times, but this on-again off-again relationship with your own children, who sometimes seem like strangers, has to be harder than your 'ex' and other people realise.

Getting into the swing of it

Here are some tips for part-time parents to help fathers (and mothers too) keep everything positive for everyone involved:

- Try to communicate amicably about everything to do with seeing the children, even if you feel you're always having to compromise – it's worth it! This probably sounds obvious but it's surprising how often parents fail here. Remember, even a controlled iciness towards one another in front of the children is unpleasant for them to handle, so it's more than just avoiding disagreements in front of them, it's being cheery that's needed.
- You'll be anxious to do everything to help them feel positive about seeing you and so naturally you'll want to take into account their reactions and opinions about the timing of their contact

with you. They'll probably want to please you and will be reassured by being able to make arrangements with you, but it's usually best to make plans with Mum before you can safely regard them as definite. This especially applies in the early period after the separation when everyone's only just getting used to things and misunderstandings are common. They'll be reassured that you and Mum can still cooperate about them, and team responsibility certainly can't work without consultation.

- We talked about who should make the decisions about arrangements in Chapter 3. Remember, if you give the children too much choice about their arrangements, you may risk them feeling they are having to make an awkward choice between two loved ones. You and Mum need to be in charge of the organising and decisions, not them, at least to begin with, and for some time if things remain a bit strained between you and Mum. But make sure you listen to what they have to say about it.

- Stick to arrangements you've made so the children don't get disappointed, and your 'ex' irritated. A bit of give and take is good too, as the best laid plans may have to be changed sometimes. In other words, don't change things for no reason, and never forget to let her know. Obvious? Yes, but often forgotten and a source of great annoyance. If you sometimes resent having to be quite so answerable to her, just remind yourself of the position the children might be put in. If she cut short her Sunday outing to be home for when you said you'd be back with the children and you don't turn up for another two hours, she'll be annoyed. The children will sense this and it puts them in an awkward position in relation to their parents – who seem to be competing for time with them and it seems impossible to please either of them! It's just the sort of scenario that you want to avoid because it can leave a nasty feeling associated with the handover from Dad to Mum. A phone call from you to warn her you're coming late could save all this.

- If the children don't come when you were expecting them, don't be too ready to think they mightn't really be sick or that Mum isn't sticking to the arrangements. Sometimes it's really quite hard to fit everything that has to be done into a week and to put the right priority on things. Try to be patient and accepting until you can get together and talk about the problem. A mutual friend you both trust can often help with discussions if they look like being a bit delicate.

- Unless you've worked out a system about belongings, make sure the children go back to Mum's place with the clothes and possessions they came with if they're staying over. A list inside their bag so you can check it with them when preparing to go, is a help, not an insult to your intelligence or an attempt to control you! This simple solution will avoid any resentment about mislaid or forgotten possessions, and she's probably right, you won't remember everything you should be sending back with them. Unfortunately many men are quite inexperienced with clothing and laundry and other domestic matters and give the impression they think they're unimportant. This can lead to ill-feeling. If your 'ex' is easy-going and unconcerned about this sort of thing, all well and good. But if you get time, sort out what's going back dirty and what's going back clean. She won't always be able to guess this, and you'll save her a lot of work, and your efforts will be appreciated.

- You can have things for them that belong at your place, things they enjoy only when they're with you. This will give them an extra sense of belonging there. Invest in some spare clothes that stay with you too. Aim to help make the whole business simple and hassle-free for the children. You'll find the whole thing easier if you are fortunate enough to have reasonably homely surroundings for yourself, or if you're living with relations. But children can cope with accommodation limitations better than you might imagine.

- Even though family times like Christmas are extra hard without the children you'd so much like to be with, try to see it all from their point of view. If they're having a great time and none of their grown-ups is feeling bitter and resentful about the arrangements, then all's well, and you must find yourself a constructive alternative to feeling lonely. Do something really different or unusual on Christmas Day so you don't dwell on the children too much. Try to be flexible about seeing the children on special days, unless there's an easy way to arrange it which suits everybody. There aren't enough days in a week for kids (especially school-aged ones) to share between two households, two sets of friends and lots of relations, and they're usually just as happy having two celebrations at different times instead of one, unless someone has made them think the real day is terribly important. Whoever heard of a child who'd settle for one party when they could have two?

- Consider the idea, if it appeals to you, of having the children for an extended period in their school holidays, when they seem ready for this. You'll find that this gives you all better opportunities to get really close and share more of the ordinary experiences together that you normally miss out on. Weekends can be a bit of a rush. It's safer to discuss any new arrangements with Mum first (see above), so as not to raise false hopes. There may be valid reasons why it mightn't be a good idea, which need some discussion first. There's no reason to feel you absolutely have to have leave from work just because you're having an extended visit from your children during their school holidays. It may well be more enjoyable if you do, but depending on your present family circumstances, the availability of your relations who'd like to spend time with your children, the extent you can enjoyably involve your children in your work, the flexibility of your working hours, etc., you may well be able to continue your life with most of its commitments while your children are with you. This may give them a much more normal and realistic experience of 'life with Dad', which they can really feel part of. You can't always drop everything to attend to your children when they come and it may not be as useful to them to only have a 'holiday' relationship with you. A happy medium is best and, especially to begin with, it's important that they feel you do have lots of time for them and don't seem too preoccupied with things that don't concern them directly.

Talking to your children

Make sure you cover up your feelings about your 'ex' when you're with the children. If you're on your own you may find this hard. They are such a direct link with memories of the past. Talk about what they want to tell you about their lives in a way that sounds interested but not interfering. As we've said elsewhere, most children don't naturally volunteer much, as they tend to be involved with the here and now, not what happened yesterday. So if they're not very forthcoming, and even sound a bit surly or uncooperative, don't worry, this is fairly normal, as experienced parents will tell you. They aren't deliberately keeping secrets.

We discussed imaginary problems in Chapter 3, and these are more likely to crop up for fathers because you're likely to feel out of touch with your children. They may not be communicating with you quite as readily as they do with their mother, and you may only now be really beginning to get to know them. So don't be tempted to read too much into the things they say or do. It's easy to think a child's chance statement or behaviour means something significant when you're not feeling very confident with them or you're anxious about how they're coping with everything and ready therefore to see signs that they're not. If you ever feel doubtful about how well Mum is looking after them you'll be on the lookout for signs of problems. Some fairly common statements are, 'I don't like Mum's boyfriend, he's not nice to me', or 'I wish I could live with you, Dad'. Sometimes Mum reports that they seem to be over-excited or over-tired after a spell with you, or you notice they seem withdrawn and silent at times. All these things have several possible explanations, many of them not especially worrying ones, or else ones you can't do anything about anyway. So don't worry too much, the children are probably managing better than you think they are. Keep things positive and fun, and if you're really concerned, start by trying to talk the problem over with Mum.

W hen I first heard from the children that they'd met Mum's new boyfriend, I must admit my ears pricked up and I was really curious to hear what they said about him. To start with they just said, 'Oh, he's OK'. But for a while they weren't quite so enthusiastic about going back to Mum's after staying with me and I thought he might be something to do with it. You can imagine how I felt when Scott said to me out of the blue, 'I don't like Mum's boyfriend Dad, he's mean'. I began imagining all sorts of things, like him getting cranky with them, even punishing them. I really worried about it for a while, but I was helpless to do anything about it except just listen for any more comments from the boys. After all, their Mum was entitled to have someone in her life now, it was bound to happen. I knew if I said anything to her, she'd probably take it the wrong way. If it was me, I probably would have. They didn't say anything more for a while, and then their Mum contacted me and said she'd like me to meet Barry since he was getting to know the kids. He seemed a nice sort of bloke and I couldn't really say he wasn't OK with the boys. They certainly seemed easy-going with him. I needn't have worried.

This father understandably misinterpreted his children's remarks and gave them too much significance, causing himself unnecessary worry. They were most likely a passing expression of their initial resentment about Barry replacing their father at their mother's side, seeing her relationship with this man as an act of infidelity and as hurtful to their father. Perhaps they felt momentarily that he came between them and their mother, taking some of the attention they were used to having themselves. They may have been expressing their anger about their parents being separated, safely blaming Barry. It was also probably a chance remark without nearly as much significance for them as it had for their doubtful Dad.

Remember what we've said so far on answering the children's questions about their family circumstances as they arise in a way that suits their age and comprehension. Keep it simple, and be sure your answers put Mum in a favourable or at least neutral light. Try to be reinforcing about the job Mum's doing in bringing up your children, when you get the opportunity to. No doubt she finds her responsibilities a bit awesome sometimes, especially if she's on her own.

Keep the whole business of your failed marriage and its consequences as low-key as you can with the children, and remind yourself and them of the good things that have come out of it. An awful lot of children don't live in a traditional nuclear family these days, and step-mothers, step-fathers, half-brothers and sisters are a pretty normal part of many children's experience. Try to keep your sadness private so the children see you as secure, enthusiastic and reliable. If you've been able to realise the fruitlessness of expecting things to be fair and the destructiveness of blaming people, then you've deservedly earned the self-respect that comes from knowing you're able to be positive, dignified and detached about your family circumstances. This'll make you feel much more in charge of things, too.

The story of Chris shows how a parent's own feelings about their marriage failure can directly affect the way the children feel about them as a parent. This is something important to watch for because unless you can see what your own feelings may be doing to your children's reactions, and take this into account, you may be heading for difficulties.

Chris and his wife had talked about their problems for some years and he thought things had improved, but she eventually insisted that they separate, assuring him that the children would still see him often. He had a rather bad reaction to being separated, having not been really ready for it and it took a while (several years in fact) to get his life positive again. When the children were with him he tended to convey to them his ongoing sadness about the breakup, satisfying his dependency on his lost family by being curious about his children's and their mother's lives, so that they felt like informers. His regular reflections on their past as a family made them feel he was blaming their Mum for spoiling his life.

They began to find their visits to him were a bit of a duty, a way of cheering Dad up, rather than for having fun with him. Quite often they felt they didn't want to go and see him when they were meant to. Chris needed more time to resolve his feelings about his marriage. The fact that he hadn't done this meant he was living only for his contact with the children. He was drawing so much from them emotionally for his own comfort that their visits had become more important for him than for them. The children were feeling they had to look after him rather than he them. The likely result, if this situation had continued, was that the children would become less and less inclined to visit their father and eventually refuse, causing all sorts of problems with Chris blaming their mother and possibly going to court over access. The story fortunately has a happy ending, because Chris found a new relationship and was able to begin a more positive new life, which didn't place such an emotional burden on the children. His new partner had quite a talent with children and was able to liven up their weekends considerably.

Keep a cheerful record of your times together, so that in years to come you can reminisce together. As they get older your children will ask themselves and you more questions about their family. You'll find it satisfying to show them all the things you did together to go on being a father, even on limited time with them, and you'll be able to have a few laughs about valuable memories. As they grow older they will be able to appreciate the continuity and commitment these memories represent.

Making good use of your time together

Try to have some interesting ideas up your sleeve about how to spend your time together. You don't have to spend a lot of money to have fun. Relationships can flourish on quietly getting on with life together, and sharing ordinary tasks. This is made easier if you have been able to set up your own home where they can feel they belong and have some territory which they feel is theirs. Children love helping with everyday things, though it may take twice as long to do the job! With a little bit of imagination, you can make very ordinary tasks into fun games, if you're prepared to give time and have patience.

Visiting relations is useful and may help you be more relaxed, especially if your kids are quite young. And your family will be reassured that your divorce has not cut the children off from their side of the family (see also Chapter 6).

Boredom can be a danger when they're away from their regular circle of friends and their more usual surroundings, or if your accommodation is limited. An activity you know they enjoy and you know they don't do at Mum's can be useful to 'have up your sleeve'. Don't make the mistake of thinking they must be constantly occupied, however. Quiet times are important and children need opportunities to learn to use their own initiative to entertain themselves, even though their time with you is limited. They should know that you have needs for rest and privacy too, and can't spend all your time together providing constant entertainment and attention. A few grumbles about 'nothing to do' or occasional restlessness won't reflect on how they feel about you or their time with you, so don't feel you have to jump to it and think of something for them whenever this happens. Periods of winding down after an outing before the next event of the day, for example, are important. These are the times for doodling, dreaming and reflecting together, perhaps out of doors, looking at a view or driving along, times when pleasant chats which make you feel warm and close sometimes just happen. They are important. In our 'hi-tech' world of instant entertainment it's easy to find that a whole weekend passes without slowing down and just 'being together'.

Don't feel you have to do or provide what they're pestering you for. Skilful parenting is about providing opportunities and experiences which children wouldn't ever have if all the ideas on how to spend the time were left to them. Steering them in new directions allows them to continually learn and extend themselves through discovering the unexpected. You certainly don't always have to do what they seem to think they want, just to keep them happy. It's a matter of keeping one step ahead of them with what you've planned, so you're in charge but striking a happy medium between their preferences and what experiences you want for them.

Resist the temptation to give them expensive treats all the time though sometimes your natural love for them will make you feel like indulging them – every time you see them it seems a pretty special occasion making you want to celebrate together! One of the dangers is that they come to expect it and may make some unfavourable comparisons between you and Mum which cause problems. She may feel she has the humdrum routine of weekday parenting, perhaps on limited finance and going out to work herself; and you have all the fun and can afford to keep giving them outings and gifts while she is struggling. She may not be able to appreciate that one of the ways you naturally want to compensate for feeling left out of their lives is to give them things to enjoy together and which will remind them of you. This happened to Doug and Anne in Chapter 1.

So don't over-do the treats and gifts. In building relationships, children usually benefit more from your time and direct attention than your money. Children want and need more than anything to have fun with you and this takes time, empathy, imagination and energy, but not necessarily money. Playing together at something simple which gives the opportunity for a few laughs and a bit of rough and tumble can make for a real sense of warmth and closeness. In Chapter 8 we talk some more about spending time with children.

Setting limits

It's often harder for a part-time parent to have the confidence to be firm. You feel as if you're being a parent in a sort of vacuum without a base line of knowledge about your children's day-to-day experience of adults; you don't know what they're used to. Perhaps in the past you tended to leave most of the everyday rules and routines to Mum and weren't all that involved. You'll probably be tempted to be pretty lenient because it seems such a shame to have confrontations during your precious time together, and because you're afraid of putting them off their visits. This is very understandable. *But it's usually a mistake to relax on discipline and standards of behaviour, because often children in fact need the structure these provide more than ever, after the upheaval in their family.* You must try to be as confident as you can when it comes to discipline. Children usually respond well to the security provided by clear statements (and reminders!) of what the rules of the household are, even though at the time they often resist them. And if you've been pretty lax to begin with, it will be much harder to tighten up your house rules later, which you'll certainly find you need to do when a new partner comes into your life.

Although it often helps to know how Mum handles the children in certain situations, don't feel you've got to do it her way to avoid confusing them. You probably won't know much about how she deals with them anyway and you'll be more out of touch as time goes on, so try to have the confidence to do what you think. Try to be yourself, explain that this is how you want things done here, and ignore any minor complaints, moodiness or resistance. This way you won't be manipulated by your children, who are well aware that you're not in a position to know what goes on at Mum's, and can get skilful at playing one parent off against the other, especially if they know you don't talk to each other much unless you have to.

When a good deal of your life is spent without children, you can forget how much longer it takes to get anything done or to get to places on time, when they have to be organised. This is especially true with younger, less independent children. It can take a long time to get away on an outing, so allow for this in your timetabling. Most children naturally don't want to stop what they're doing in order to do something a grown-up is telling them to do like get ready for something. So don't expect instant compliance with a direction to 'find your shoes', or 'clean your teeth' etc., and allow plenty of time for these essentials so you don't end up getting impatient and tense. Expect to have to chivvy children regularly about things like mealtimes, bedtimes, tidying up etc.; it's a normal part of parenting to have to nag a bit!

If your child seems reluctant to return to Mum's after a holiday with you, don't be tempted to think anything's wrong there. It's much more likely to be that they had such a good time that they want more, or they are expressing sadness at having to part from you, and feel reluctant to resume the usual term-time routine that has to be associated with life at Mum's place. The way to handle this is to say a few reassuring and positive things like what a great time you've had, what fun it might be if life were all holidays and that next time will come quicker than you think, etc. In other words, be positive about what they're going back to but acknowledge that partings are sad. Whatever your hopes might be that they could stay and live with you and however much you wish they didn't have to go, avoid putting across any doubt about what must happen.

At least until they are teenagers, it's dangerous for children to get the feeling they have a choice about such a major thing as who they mainly live with. Being too open about how much you wish your children could be with you all the time can sound as if there's an ongoing competition for them between their parents. You may be making them feel they could influence events, have a choice between one parent at the expense of the other. This is dangerous ground, so we refer to it again later. Major changes should be discussed and prepared for by you two parents together, perhaps with a counsellor, well before any doubts about the future are communicated to a younger child.

When you find it difficult to accept things about your children when they visit, don't make the mistake of thinking that the way they are with you necessarily reflects the way they are (and presumably are allowed to be) at Mum's place. It may be, especially if there are quite long gaps between their visits to you, that they're just trying you out to re-establish the basc linc of what's acceptable to you, a way of checking out forgotten rules. And they may be excited to see you and so forgetful of, say, their manners. *Don't waste any time thinking to yourself, what are my children turning into away from my influence and standards? Just get on with asserting yours in a kindly but persuasive way.* Try to think of it as potentially useful and enriching for children to grow up knowing first hand that there's more than one way of doing things. The chances are it will be if you manage to run your household in a way which never implies any criticism of or challenge to your children's other home. This is a much more positive and helpful approach than being disappointed.

Staying in charge of your children by setting sensible limits is so important that we continue with this in Chapter 7.

Including others

If any of your children are quite young and/or you don't feel very confident about looking after them for any length of time on your own, don't feel you're failing them (or yourself) if you involve relations in helping you get used to being with them without their Mum.

Don't be in too much of a hurry to introduce your girlfriend to the children, however keen you and she might be to do this. If she looks like being part of your life for a while, involve her in a low-key way to start with, making sure you still have plenty of time with the children yourself. The right timing will depend on how long ago you separated and how well integrated into their lives their contact with you is, how well your 'ex' is really able to accept the replacement you've found for her, and whether she herself has a new relationship. The children may resent your friend to begin with if she seems to them to be taking too much of your attention from them, and they're likely to object to her occupying their mother's place in relation to you for quite a while after your separation. She's a living reminder that you and their Mum aren't going to get back together, and you may not realise how long children go on hoping for this despite what seem like very obvious improvements all round as a result of you being separated. Children can be quite rejecting and mischievous towards potential step-mothers. (We shall be thinking about ideal ways of timing introductions in the next chapter, 'Step-families'.)

If the children are encouraged to get to know and like your new friend and she turns out to be one of a series of partners in your life, they may come to have little faith and confidence in making friends with adults, because they keep disappearing out of their lives. Avoid letting the children come to count on the things she and they do together at the weekends unless you're pretty sure your relationship with her is going to last. If you couldn't keep your marriage going for the sake of the children, then you certainly won't want to keep an affair going for that reason, and repeated experiences of being left by loved people won't help the children.

You can work out a happy medium about what's going to work and what might cause problems. *If you know Mum will find it hard to accept you having a new lover then the chances are the children will find it a bit hard too, so it may be worth keeping your new relationship low-key for a while to give your 'ex' time to feel more detached and accepting about this.* Some people are very resentful of their 'ex's' new partner and remain so for some time. If Mum is feeling this way about your girlfriend, it's very likely that your children will have taken up some of her feelings about this person. Don't blame them or try too hard to change the way they feel. They can't help being in the position they are, and what they need is time to get used to everyone at their own pace, not pressure to change their views so they conflict with those of their mother.

Of course this doesn't mean you have to 'lock up' your girlfriends, and they can be a very useful addition to your family activities. Children need to meet people who are important to you. If you are sharing your home, your bed and your life with somebody it's usually a mistake to conceal the fact except temporarily. Surprisingly, despite behaving initially as if they thought the opposite (see above), children are often happier once they know their parents have someone new (as long as they don't think this relationship caused the breakup), because they no longer have to worry about their loneliness. *You* must decide what seems a natural and sensible way of handling your parenting responsibilities and your love life in a way which doesn't complicate things too much for the children. Once again it's a matter of being one step ahead of things by being aware of how your life may seem from your children and your 'ex's' points of view, regardless of whether their points of view are reasonable to you. Use your common sense and sensitivity, without being too serious about it all!

Don't forget to look after your new partner's feelings about your 'appendages' from the past turning up regularly to be part of your lives for a while. Talk to her about her reactions to them regularly, in a way that encourages her to feel it's OK not to like every aspect of the package deal she's got involved in. They'll take some adjusting to, especially if she isn't already a parent herself.

When there's another 'father'

Don't worry about Mum's new partner taking over your role as a father. It may hurt you terribly that he sees more of your children than you do, or that they call him 'Dad' and not you. Naturally this brings fears of being replaced, because there is the potential for a close relationship developing based on daily contact with a male adult who is close to Mum. But this relationship will not be a rival one unless you adults are in conflict about it. You are unlikely to be replaced in their hearts as father unless you withdraw from your own commitment to the children. Try to be thankful that he's making the children's mother happy and that this is good for them. See this person as an addition to your children's lives rather than a complication. *If you can give your children joyful and positive experiences regularly and try to see this time as separate and special for you all, there's no reason to think that the children will necessarily be confused or divided by having 'two fathers', especially if all of you are communicating about the children amicably when it's necessary.*

Keeping going

In the still of the night you'll probably sometimes feel it's all an incredible effort, an uncomfortable tie which governs your social and working life. You'll ask yourself whether it's really all worth it. This part-time parenting seems like all give, and you don't seem to get much closeness back. Your children feel like strangers, and you can't feel involved when you don't know anything about most of their lives. Perhaps they only come and see you out of a sense of duty and not out of a real sense of belonging to you. You can't identify readily with some of the characteristics you see emerging in them as they grow older, characteristics you would like to have 'counter-influenced'. You feel like only a half-parent.

Take heart. Children looking back on the experience of their parents' divorce often say that the one thing that made the whole business easier to bear was being free to go on seeing the parent they didn't live with most of the time. They need you. If your relationship with your former partner is able to be cooperative for the sake of the lives you produced together, and you're doing half the things suggested here, then in the long run it'll be well worth the effort it sometimes seems. And it'll be fun. Children can develop strong bonds with a parent they don't spend all that much time with, especially if that time is spent well, and even if they have several other parent figures in their lives. Blood ties are strong and although you may sometimes feel concerned at the apparent importance of a step-father in your child's life, provided you are 'doing your bit', your child will never lose sight of the significance and value of their 'real' Dad.

You certainly are contributing usefully to how your children cope with their ongoing disapppointment that you didn't stay together, as well as providing them with enriching experiences and perspectives they wouldn't otherwise have had. And you are ensuring that they don't grow up thinking that they have a father who isn't interested in them, and in doubt about their own worth because they lost a valued relationship. You won't have another chance to be part of your children's youth.

5

Step-families

From the time you separate onwards it'll be more and more likely that the two households your children are now part of will contain more people than just their parents. Of course there may have been someone else in either of your lives, with or without children of their own, for quite some time. The children had to get used to everybody straight away, and maybe had to accept the idea of one of their parents taking on someone else's children because they fell in love with that someone else. Either way, people other than parents in your children's two homes are obviously going to have a significant bearing on how it all works.

The chances are all the new additions to your children's lives will be more difficult for the adults to adjust to than it will be for the children. Certainly the timing of introductions and the explanations given to everybody will have a direct bearing on how the children react to newly-forming families and how quickly they adjust. So again, you can make it easier and happier for everyone by the way you handle it, if you take control.

The first step is to work out how you feel about new relationships and responsibilities and how honest and realistic you're being about what you're taking on. And, as always, try to see it all from the children's angle, so you can be one step ahead in anticipating their reactions and feelings.

New partnerships and good timing

It must be said that it's probably easier for children if they have a chance to adjust to their parents being separated for a period of time before their parents take new partners. They often feel that this new person has taken the other parent's rightful position beside their Mum or Dad, and are sad that this means the parent has already been replaced and reconciliation is ruled out. It's a matter of trying to ensure that your children don't have to get used to too much all at once – their parents no longer living together is hard enough! And for you, although being on your own isn't usually much fun (we all need mental and physical companionship), it's often better in the long run if you don't go straight into another involved relationship. To make a better go of it next time, you need time to reflect on what really went wrong and what you really want and need out of a relationship. It's usually easier to do this when you aren't involved with anyone, so you have a sort of 'time out' to collect your thoughts. If you have a period of being 'unattached', you can make good use of it to learn more about yourself.

This is all very well in theory, but emotions, especially those concerned with romance, aren't usually amenable to much forward planning or strategic timing. Very often a new relationship is itself the impetus for deciding to separate, whether or not this is ideal for the children, and a new person, presenting new dilemmas for the children, is around from the word go. A new partner has a way of inflaming the already aroused emotions of the partner who feels cheated (remember the days of 'co-respondents'?). This can make things much harder for the children, who will be likely to attribute fault to the parent who's found someone new, to give themselves an explanation for the separation, and out of loyalty and sympathy for the 'wronged parent'. Just because we're supposed to be more accepting of and enlightened about love relationships these days and the concept of fault has been formally removed from divorce proceedings, it certainly doesn't mean we're any better at handling the emotions of jealousy, anger, feeling betrayed and cheated, all of which can run riot at times, even when you're trying your hardest to have a 'civilised' separation for the sake of the children. Keeping the emotional complications of a new partnership till later can make things easier, as well as give you useful time.

If the timing of a new relationship has already taken care of itself, keep an extra eye out for children's reactions to it all and try to make them feel they can talk to you about it without feeling threatened. They need to sort out their feelings about their changed family circumstances. Children can feel quite resentful about relationships suddenly 'forced' on them without notice or discussion.

W e really felt left out when we heard Dad was getting married. We'd only met her once or twice and none of us had really got to know her. Dad just announced it to us and it made me feel that a whole lot of things had been happening – plans being made – behind my back, which were going to affect me. Would I have to act as if she were a mother? Would she want to change all the furniture round in *our* house? Would they want to be private together at times when we would have normally had Dad to ourselves? It made us feel uncertain right from the beginning about whether it'd work out, and looking back on it now, I know we must have made it hard for her. I think it's easier in this situation if you can get to know the person really well so you can feel part of what's going on, have time to get used to it, not just have it dumped on you as if your feelings were irrelevant.

If you're wondering what's the best way to handle bringing a new person into your children's lives before actually doing it, consider the following:

1. Have the children got an agreeable set of arrangements for seeing both their Mum and Dad, which they've had a chance to get used to and is going along nicely?

2. Have you discussed the children with your new friend fully and got an idea how they feel about them and how you're going to deal with issues like discipline and standards?

3. Have you planned together how you're going to define the person's status in your life and how you're going to explain it to the children?

4. How is your 'ex' likely to react to your having found someone else?

The answers to all these questions will help you decide whether the time has come, and considering them in advance will definitely help you avoid some difficulties.

However much you may fear the reaction of your 'ex' to someone new in your life, it's best to tell them yourself rather than let them find out through the children, and especially if you're uncertain how the news will be received. Part-time fathers might bear in mind that time with the children is meant for Dad and them, so when girlfriends are around giving you a hand, make sure especially in the early stages of your visiting routine you don't risk the children feeling that your 'Mum replacement' – and this is how they'll see her – is more important to you than they are.

Making it known

After all these points that sound like warnings, don't feel that new relationships must be kept secret or necessarily postponed indefinitely! Children should be encouraged to accept that their parents have needs for love, intimacy and companionship that are separate from their own interests. If Mum has someone new, often the children are relieved when Dad has too (or the other way round, time-wise). They can stop worrying about Dad and how he's managing on his own now that he's got someone to look after him like Mum has! Introductions of course should be low-key so the children can accept him or her at their own pace and no awkward expectations are issued about how they should feel about this person. Discuss your intentions about new relationships with the children in a way that makes them feel they are in on your decisions (see above), you considered their feelings and opinions, and that nothing which is about to directly affect them has been decided without reference to them. Tell them why you like this person and how you see them fitting in. You are not seeking their permission of course, but rather making them feel involved, accepting their reactions (yes, even the negative ones) in an understanding way.

A house move at the same time as you start a new family grouping can help – everyone starts off on a more equal footing and no established territory is invaded. It's easier to set new ground rules when everyone is, in a sense, making a new beginning.

It's best when a new partnership is to be made formal that the children aren't the ones to carry the news between their two households. You mightn't think that getting married is going to make all that much difference if the person has been part of your life for a while, but children are often surprisingly aware of the change of status your partner is going to have. And if parents can communicate with each other directly about major family events, they communicate openness and authority, showing that they can be team parents despite the circumstances (see also Chapter 4).

The special challenges

All the different combinations of relationships that are possible in a step-family, without even contemplating the complex combinations resulting from third or subsequent marriages, mean that they really are different from 'biological' families. Whatever their makeup, they have several basic characteristics that make them different, extra dimensions which are best looked in the eye from the beginning. These things need to be considered in a realistic way when embarking on blended family life – but unfortunately they often aren't. Lots of people in step-families say later on that they wished they had approached it all differently, they didn't know it would be this hard to adjust or where to look for advice. These are some of the things that need acknowledging:

- Step-families are headed by a couple who didn't have time together before children arrived. Getting to know each other as a couple without other responsibilities is no guarantee of a successful partnership of course, but the gradual arrival of children is definitely easier to adjust to. The chances of your working as a team about them are higher because there are no established alliances or unfamiliar personalities to adjust to. The adjustment to a 'package deal' family is even harder for someone who isn't already a parent.

- They contain relationships that have often been created suddenly and without choice. Your step-children didn't choose to have you in their lives, they're stuck with you (and maybe your children too) because of something they'd rather hadn't happened. Someone's going to feel this way about it some of the time because it's a fact, and this has to be a bad start to living together. Why should you like each other? You don't know much about each other's history and personalities, warts and all, but suddenly you're all together trying to get along.

- The members (some of them anyway) are linked by ties which we tend to see as less worthy of respect than blood ties. This paves the way for authority problems, the 'I won't cooperate with you, you're not my real father' kind.

- Added to this there's a whole lot of step-mythology left over from the days when parents died younger. Almost all of it is negative and so it fosters unfavourable comparisons between adults, and makes further opportunities for manipulation and rejection of authority. It's part of human nature that we tend to just accept and enjoy the good parts of people, but look for causes and place blame for the things we don't like about them, sometimes using them as excuses for things not being quite how we'd like them to be.

- There are bonds between members created as a result of a previous marriage which can create awkward alliances in step-families. A parent often becomes closer to their biological child after a breakup. This can be a threat to the new couple because there's a 'he's my child, not yours' mentality operating.

- When there's only a small age difference between members whose status in the family places them in different generations, there are always some extra emotional dynamics. A Mum with small children might marry a dad with same-aged grandchildren and herself be younger than his children. Mum with teenage daughters might partner a younger fellow seen as romantically eligible by his stepdaughters. Nowadays we tend to kid ourselves that this generational overlap is normal and acceptable, but our sense of order about families is still very traditional underneath our modern accepting ideas, and the strains and tensions caused by this aspect of remarriages can be quite powerful.

- Step-families created after a divorce rather than a death face the special challenge of ongoing links with a former, now obsolete family. This means everyone has to live with the past a bit, and some with a history that they weren't ever part of. A step-parent has a potential rival in relation to the children elsewhere, someone whose relationship with the children is supposed to be nurtured and encouraged. This is a complication many step-family couples sometimes have to admit they could do without. In many ways it's less complicated when the new partnership follows the death of a parent. The boundaries of responsibility for the step-parent are clearer and there isn't this ongoing focus for affection, loyalty or resentment outside the new family unit.

These influences are obviously not present in 'original families'. They are potential stresses which are often overlooked by the newly-formed couple in their natural enthusiasm to improve on their past marriage(s) and their joy at starting over. Unfortunately, second marriages don't have a much better track record than first ones. But they are just as popular. They are usually embarked upon, after a failure, with particularly high hopes, but with far more challenges to be overcome.

Optimism is great, and we really should be looking at all the issues we've mentioned and saying it's terrific that we're doing so well under the circumstances! But unless optimism is combined with realistic attitudes about the past and the future, it can turn into disappointment and frustration. *Being positive and good-humoured about your situation needs to include honestly acknowledging real issues and feelings, and addressing them constructively.*

But also beware taking family problems too seriously by blaming them on the step-family factor. First and foremost step-families are families, and so they are confronted with the same joys, frustrations and disappointments as any family. There are plenty of biological families where relationships are conflict-ridden and destructive. Leaving this sort of family and starting again is a positive move towards a better situation for your children, provided the extra complexities of life in a blended family are appreciated.

Who should be responsible for what

In biological families there is an implicit, unquestioned sense of order about matters of discipline, boundaries of responsibility and level of involvement which guides family life. When children have a 'real' parent somewhere else and live in a step-family, there are no predetermined ground rules about who's in charge of what. Or how close step-parents should get to children who have biological parents, one they've teamed up with, one they've 'replaced'. How much authority should they have? Should they be a substitute parent, or take a back seat? And so on. The extent of your involvement with your stepchildren will naturally depend very much on whether they live with you most of the time or visit you regularly. And whether you have your own children by a former marriage or by your current one.

Most step-parents, if they're being honest, are uncertain about how much to be a parent towards step-children, wanting to be (out of love for one of their parents) but lacking the emotional investment in them that comes from having been part of their lives from the beginning. How shall I be with this child, how do I pitch it right for them and for me, they wonder? There's more about other people's children in Chapter 6.

Parents must decide how much they want their new partner to do with the children, whether they want to go on looking after most of their needs themselves, protecting their new partner from the past, at least to begin with, and from too much involvement with the children too soon. Some fathers are only too glad for their new partner to take on a mothering role with their children right from the beginning and this will certainly tend to happen if she has her own children – it will seem artificial if she doesn't. Role boundaries, to use the jargon, are easier for caretaking mothers, since they traditionally do more of the parenting in any family, at least when the children are young. Their main concern will be how to define their new partner's relationship with the children so he is involved in a comfortable way which doesn't seem to them like a 'takeover' of their father's role.

Since there are no preset rules it's up to you two to make them, and you must do this together. Perhaps you started thinking about this before you all moved in together. Depending on the regularity of contact the children have with their 'other' parent, and whether you have your own children living with you most of the time, you should be able to work out a way of operating. Most importantly you need to be honest with yourself about what sort of relationship is going to suit you, what your partner is prepared to go on contributing or undertake to begin contributing, what will reinforce rather than undermine the children's relationship with the other parent, etc. *If you don't address boundaries of responsibilities and matters of policy and discipline from the beginning, it may be harder to introduce changes later.*

Making room for everybody

Assuming that for most readers both natural parents are actively involved in children's lives, the new couple must leave plenty of 'room' for the real parent. Mums should not assume their children will accept and continue with the new man the way they do with the 'real' but often absent Dad. Make the new relationship seem like an interesting extra, rather than a substitute one. The new partner needs to be a sort of understudy parent, in the background, but ready. Let him and your children get to know each other as people, not as your appendages, at their own pace, not yours. Be wary of trying to speed up their acceptance of him because you're anxious for them to like him just because you do. This is a common mistake. But don't go to the other extreme so that he feels excluded from family life, like an outsider in what's now his own home as much as everybody else's. Also watch out that in your new pleasure at having a partner again you don't make the children feel excluded, with your enthusiasm to make him feel important and accepted. Remember that the scene is set for the children to feel he's a bit of an interloper anyway. You must balance your loyalties and affections skilfully.

Step-fathers (and for step-mothers see Chapter 6) should go easy on discipline and issuing policy and rules in the early stages, but should show clear support for Mum on these matters. It's a good idea to be a bit reserved with physical contact, as it communicates intimacy, which children will accept and respond to only when they're ready. So go easy on hair-plaiting, neck-washing, hugs and contact play until you sense they're ready for it.

If you can organise a low-key way for all the parents and step-parents to get together with all the children, not regularly, just once will do, this can be a useful demonstration to the children that you're all a team on the same side in relation to them. In other words, don't avoid each other because of the past. *If you've accepted everything about how this new family came to be and what aspects of the past will continue to be part of it, then the chances are the children are going to accept it all too, given consideration and time.* You really will be a 'blended' family.

What should we call ourselves?

Names and titles can be a sore point, if there's a lingering fear of a takeover by a 'replacement' parent, or a step-parent is overkeen to be seen as as good as a child's 'real' parent. The important thing from the point of view of children's needs and feelings is that they know who everybody really is, and this won't necessarily be reflected in what titles they use for everybody. Long before children understand any biology, they form a notion of the importance of blood ties or kinship links. They need to know how they are related to everyone, however much or little time they spend with them. After all, a relationship with another person exists, however remote they might be or seem from day-to-day. So tell them how their families are made up, and explain it in a way that is simple, open and allows them to develop their own way of incorporating everyone into their lives at their own pace. Parents, especially those who don't see their children as much as they'd like to, are naturally keen to be referred to by the label that seems to say that this is how my children think of me, despite my absence from their daily lives. It's reassuring for a father to be called 'Dad' every fortnight, especially when his children have a step-father they see everyday. But don't insist on them using the names you want to hear for your own reasons.

First names all round for adults as well as children are often easier and aren't controversial or ambiguous. They save having to draw attention to a child's status in the family, when introductions are made. Introducing your step-child at a social function doesn't require you to explain whether or not they're a blood relation, neither should it require you to disguise the absence of a biological relationship. Saying, 'I'd like you to meet Jamie', invites the person to accept Jamie for who he is and allows Jamie the freedom to feel valued for himself, not for his relationships. Children who call their step-mother 'Mum' aren't in doubt about who she is, she just feels Mum-like at the time. Don't think of correcting them, because they haven't got it wrong. Children can have two Dads and two Mums, without forgetting the real status of each of them. Their varying use of names doesn't necessarily reflect any passing weakening or strengthening of ties. The names we use spontaneously usually reflect how close we feel at the time. Once children can readily address a step-parent by their agreed-upon name, they have integrated that adult as part of their family. There's no harm in saying what you like being called without making a big deal of it, if the subject comes up. Insisting on children calling their step-parents 'Mum' and 'Dad' (very special titles for very special people) can create division and antagonism about what may already be a somewhat forced relationship for them.

Surnames can be the focus of a different kind of concern between families. It's almost always best when both natural parents are involved with their children and everybody is managing this happily, that the children keep their original surname. You probably don't think twice about this. After all, if they're with Dad regularly, why should his name be struck out just because Mum got married again to someone who's also going to be important to the child, though in a different way? A surname is an important statement about your identity and origins, and need not be a source of conflict, doubt or rivalry just because a child now lives with children who have different surnames.

A new baby

New babies have a way of consolidating a relationship, especially in a family where one or both of you have your own children by someone else. You want to have one that's 'ours' as well as having 'yours' and 'mine'. You'll remember from before, though, that they take a lot of time and can change the routine of family life considerably, so watch out (discreetly) for how it's affecting your other children and stepchildren. They won't appreciate feeling you're so absorbed in the new baby that you imply the newcomer is more important to you than they are because this child is the only one who belongs to both of you. Become aware of the potential in your words and actions for the usual sibling rivalry, this time with icing on top! Without making too much of it all, involve your older children in the event in a positive way and once baby has arrived, try to have life go on much as usual in most respects, encouraging them to help with baby, but not demanding that they do.

I was pretty sure that Sam was glad that his Dad had remarried because his Mum had, but I was really glad we had a girl first. I was a bit worried that he might feel he'd been replaced in his Dad's affections if we'd had a son. Sam seemed quite interested in and accepting of his sister and said he hoped we'd have a boy next and then another girl, so there'd be two of each! We did go on to have a son, and everything is fine.

Grandparents

Grandparents are an important aspect of a child's sense of their origins and therefore their identity. The importance of the link is two-way, of course, and one of the immediate fears, particularly for paternal grandparents, when there's a separation in the family with young children involved, is the possibility of losing touch with grandchildren. This needn't and shouldn't happen especially when there has been an ongoing relationship to date. Help carry on these links as naturally as possible.

Seldom mentioned, though, is the position of people we have to call 'step-grandparents' for want of a better title. They probably will become involved to some extent in the lives of their children's stepchildren as time goes on, and can play a useful part in reinforcing the status of a step-parent if they are allowed to be included as grandparents. It might seem cumbersome indeed for a child to have eight grandparents, but explanations and occasional contact are enough for a sense of family to be reinforced in a child's mind and for an enjoyable link with a step-parent's family to be made. Any awkwardness or ambiguity in the role to be taken with a step-grandchild is likely to be in the minds of grown-ups. Children will accept who everyone is because they know about people having parents. Ideally of course grandparents should welcome the new family member, recognising the new partner's position and treating the new juniors not so much as grandchildren but as children who, like any others, need and enjoy love and time together.

I had to smile to myself when I overheard my four-year-old daughter having what seemed to be a competition with her 'half-brother' (he's ten and lives with his mother, who has remarried) about which of them had the most cousins. They carefully counted them all out in turn, including his step-father's nieces and nephews (none of our family has ever met them or is ever likely to). He also unhesitatingly included my sister's children and so he got the higher score and 'won'. But he seemed to have had no doubts about his relationship with everyone in his extended family. As an afterthought he decided his half-sister (my daughter) should include his step-father's relations in her list because, after all, if they had all those other cousins in common and they were brother and sister, then these must be her cousins too! It was a game of course, but it showed how matter-of-factly he had absorbed all the different branches of his family, extended through remarriages.

Positive attitudes for successful step-families

Here's how to create a happy and blended step-family:

1. Look after yourselves as a couple. Talk openly together, asking each other lots of questions about how you think you'll each react to inevitable situations before they arise. Establish a routine for settling family disputes before they get serious. Make a point of taking time out regularly as a couple to discuss family issues, so you can be united as a couple. Even when you're so busy you neglect issues that you know need discussing, acknowledge what's come up so it can be noted for later if not resolved immediately. Acknowledge that your relationship has extra pressure to withstand, even though you have some experience behind you. Each of you needs to feel secure about the strength of your relationship so you convey your solidarity as a couple to the children. They are more likely to accept and respect a step-parent who is a secure member of the partnership that heads the family. We talked about the importance of couple solidarity in Chapter 2. It's as important for happy functioning in step-families as it is for the to and fro factor.

2. Take your time in adjusting to new relationships, remembering that there's nothing to say you must love your partner's children any more than you must love his sister or parents, though of course it does help if they're lovable at least sometimes! Similarly, don't expect your new partner to automatically like your children just because they're yours. Make sure your partner can talk about the children to you and find you accepting of their feelings.

3. Don't expect instant emergence of clearcut parental feelings about the children, or acceptance from them. Everybody's expectations of your role in the family (not to mention your own) will put pressure on you to adjust more quickly than is really feasible, so take each day at a time and accept that you will feel ambivalent about your family quite often.

4. Expect and be prepared to weather some bad feelings about you from the step-children and even from your own children as they adjust to things. Try to acknowledge their feelings, but don't accept rudeness. Be prepared to give some sensible detached guidance about relationships and feelings, pitched to suit their ages of course. These are real issues and it'll be worth the courage it sometimes needs to get things out in the open. They won't necessarily just take care of themselves.

5. Do all you both can to foster the children's relationship with their largely absent parent. Your family is not neatly contained within your home, there is an influential adult elsewhere who is an ongoing part of your lives. The visiting regime, whether it's children coming or children going, will sometimes seem like an intrusion. But the children will adjust more quickly to their new family if their relationship with both their parents remains strong and they feel you're helping it to be. This will only happen if everyone in the new family really feels positive about the children's permanent links with their past family.

6. Being positive includes containing your inevitable frustrations in front of the children, avoiding comparisons, being interested without being inquisitive about their relationship with their absent parent and what they do together, not trying to take over all maternal or paternal responsibilities so the children feel you want to replace their parent, etc. Accept that you may have mixed feelings about the claim your step-children's absent parent has when you are doing all you can to provide a loving and nurturing new environment for them, along with all the hard work that involves. Above all, be easy-going and accommodating about this aspect of family life, conveying that you accept it unquestioningly (even if you don't always), and seeing the advantages of it wherever you can.

7. Try to ignore any suspicions that may emerge that your children might actually enjoy their step-parent more than their 'real' parent, or become closer to them as time goes on. Don't let this affect your positive approach to these two different and complementary relationships. A child needs freedom (freedom from your inhibiting anxieties and hopes, that is) to form their own kind of bond with the people who are important in their lives.

8. Visiting children are guests as well as family, but don't make too much of a special occasion too often when your own or your partner's children are visiting. Let them fit into the family routine much as it is, at the same time making them feel they belong and aren't just visitors. If the age range (and therefore interest range) isn't too wide, do some things that can involve everybody. This will help prevent children making comparisons about who is more important to whom, as well as exposing them to life at your place as it really is.

9. Make sure you each allow the other time alone with your biological children sometimes. This reinforces their special

bond and gives you either time alone with yours or valuable time on your own.

10. Try not to treat the two sets of children differently on matters of discipline or favours. You're bound to feel differently about them but aim for this not to show too much.

11. Expect there to be some tensions between the two sets of children. They don't have to like each other, just adjust to each other so they can get along. If they are younger when you join forces, they most probably will accept each other easily, but this doesn't happen so readily with older children, especially after the initial novelty has worn off.

12. Try to be confident, clear and consistent about your expectations of everybody, so everyone knows where they stand with you. Don't feel you always have to cover up feelings of frustration or rejection and alienation within the family. Express yourself and your needs accordingly, tuned accurately to the ages and feelings of the children and taking care not to be destructive or hurtful. And be sure you listen and accept (not necessarily encourage) the children's feelings and demands.

6

Part-time Step-parents

We've seen how people who get involved together when either of them already has children are taking on quite a challenge. There are some extra issues for women who team up with men who have ex-wives and children, issues which don't usually affect step-fathers in quite the same way.

It's easier in many ways if his children live with you all the time, as your parenting responsibility towards them is more clear cut. But having them visit you regularly while they live mainly with their Mum is the much more common situation. So this time it's really part-time mothers who get a chapter of their own.

Contemplating a 'package deal'

One of the reasons why embarking on a new life as part of a blended family raises particular issues for step-mothers, is because we women are 'programmed' to home-make and parent by virtue of our gender, so that it's all supposed to come naturally. But parenting someone else's children, those of your favourite man, doesn't always come easily, though being the mother of your own helps. At least you're familiar with children. But of course this brings a whole extra dimension to consider – being a mother to two 'sets' of children who have different kinds of relationships with you.

Making a commitment to a relationship is a big decision in itself. But when it involves not only you and your partner, but also your children, his children, and sometimes both, then the responsibility is huge, as the lives of a number of other people are going to be directly and permanently affected. So you've probably thought long and hard about what you're getting into, whether his children will like you, whether your children will get on with his, whether they will all accept the child you're going to have together, and how all these relationships will fare in the future. If you love this man, you'll naturally want to love and be loved by his children; and want him and his children to like yours. Having made the big decision to join forces, you'll be keen to meet the challenges of parenting in a blended family with flying colours. You can, but be wary if you're thinking it'll be plain sailing, because, as we've seen, step-families *are* different.

When I first moved in with John I was really keen to get into the swing of his kids coming for weekends regularly, and I put a lot of effort into trying to make them feel at home with me there too, attending to all the usual motherly things, the feminine touches to family life. I can see now that I was a bit too caught up in the novelty of my new role, wanting so much to please John, to show that I accepted his past. But I tried to do too much, and it wasn't necessary or even noticed half the time. The kids just burst into our lives at regular intervals and totally dominated every minute of our waking hours, or so it seemed to me.

John and I both work full time and usually all I really want at weekends is to be relaxed with him, not flat out keeping everybody happy. But at least they seem to accept me, even though I don't always find it easy to accept them, feeling they intrude a lot more than I'd thought they would on my life with John. And their mother is always asking us to take them at other times when she's got something else on. I know this should be nothing but a pleasure for us, but sometimes I feel like a bit of a convenience, expected to be ready and willing, often without much notice, to take over their care whenever it suits her to be without the kids. I find it hard to discuss it all frankly with John because I feel guilty about complaining about his children and I think I should be managing better. I guess new step-mothers get over these feelings in time.

You'll probably have introduced your children to him and seen how they get along together already, and certainly as soon as you and he started to get serious. Hopefully you've been able to talk frankly and honestly together about the fact that you're a 'package deal' and that if he wants you, he'll have to take on your children too. Assuming that your children see their father regularly, then you'll have thought about what sort of a role in the family your new partner is going to have with your children once you're really all together, the sorts of things we discussed in Chapter 5.

Some aspects of getting to know someone else's children are the same whether you're step-mother or step-father. Others are different and more complicated, especially when there are young children involved, because they're often more closely bonded with their female parent. Because women tend to be (and are expected to be) closer to children than men, it's harder in many ways to be a step-mother than it is to be a step-father. How are you supposed to be an on-again, off-again mother to these children who already have a mother who looks after them most of the time? Is there really room for you? Should you really be leaving all the parenting to their father?

Getting started as a step-mother

Early on in your relationship with your step-children especially, it's best to be responsive but in a low-key way, being cheery and easygoing. Their visits are primarily for them to be with their father, after all, even though you are an important part of his life. Remember this particularly if you become involved in the children's contact with Dad very soon after his separation and they haven't fully adjusted to the idea of having an occasional Dad. Let them set the pace of how quickly you become friends, without being remote or standoffish, of course. Be yourself from the beginning. *Children are remarkably astute and will respond to you best if you're genuine and straight in your approach to them*, always bearing in mind their likely point of view about you and what you stand for. If you let yourself worry too much about their reactions to you and whether they are accepting you, you're likely to come across as tentative and uneasy. They'll sense your self-consciousness and see through your valiant efforts to please and be nice all the time for the efforts they are, and you won't seem genuine.

Don't worry too much if the children seem uncommunicative or even a bit resentful of you. Let them be like this, but don't withdraw yourself, or accept outright rudeness. To begin with, before they've really got to know you and what you have to offer, they *will* resent you because you are the living proof that their parents aren't going to get back together again, which is most likely what they want. They may test you out with practical jokes and hurtful remarks, so try not to lose your patience or your sense of humour, they are probably *trying* to undermine you! If you and their Dad know that Mum hasn't yet accepted him having a new partner and she frankly disapproves of you, the children will be more likely to resent you and look out for your defects. You'll probably then find it's best to tread extra carefully over taking on too much mothering too soon. Let Dad do most of the parenting, taking a back seat for a bit longer.

Let their father take the helm most of the time when it comes to discipline and routine anyway, especially early on and if the children don't come all that often. When there's an issue or exchange directly between you and one or all of them, try to be quietly confident and firm in responding the way you think is right, without requiring strict compliance to a whole lot of details and routines which may not be all that important. Try not to impose on the family your own house rules just because you've always done it that way.

Think about the rules you want accepted. Stick to them or give them away depending on whether you think they are rational, fair, necessary to family safety, show consideration, etc. Be prepared to make some concessions, like insisting that bedroom doors are kept closed if they won't tidy up as often as you think they should. Restrain your creative desire to rearrange and refurbish territory they might regard as particularly theirs, if you're moving into a home they already feel they're an established part of with their father.

Don't be too frustrated if at first you don't get instant compliance with a request, as they may want to try you out to see what you're made of. Part of their resentment of you is because of their feeling that you've no right to tell them what to do. Stand firm gracefully and don't take the 'you're not my mother' remarks or attitudes too much to heart. But do try not to fall into the trap of making too many allowances and holding back on discipline because of 'the situation', or because you're anxious to be liked.

In the long run, children respond better and show more respect if they know exactly what you expect of them and you are consistent about it. This doesn't mean you have to be consistent with their mother's way of doing things. It can be helpful to know a bit about how she handles her children, but you probably won't get the chance to consult much with her. You don't even have to be completely consistent with their Dad – you are individuals as well as a partnership, after all – although one set of rules per household is easier for everyone and prevents adults being manipulated so easily.

You'll find it helpful if you acknowledge that you're at a disadvantage compared to their Mum and Dad because you don't know these children's past experience and all the things that have shaped their personality from the beginning. Yours is an instant relationship without the established bond that comes from having been part of their lives from the start. So don't expect to get on instantly, you haven't got the ongoing trust that exists with this special sort of bond but a kind of bond will come in time.

I often find myself wondering how to pitch things right with my step-son Dan even though he's been coming to stay with us for years now. I think it's partly because there have to be quite long gaps between his visits because of distance and we all get out of touch. I keep wanting to know how his mother would deal with this or that situation, and yet it's not as if I'd want to do the same, just that I'd feel more confident if I knew what he was used to. There's never much I can do except have the courage to use my commonsense and do what I think's best. His father's and my children are a fair bit younger so it's partly that I'm a bit inexperienced with older children and so I hesitate.

Last time he stayed, on the evening before he had to leave I was undecided about how to handle packing up his belongings. This sort of chore quite naturally usually falls to me to take care of in our household, rather than his father, and I don't question this. I didn't want to pay too much attention to the business of packing because it signified his going which we were all feeling sad about, wishing he could stay on. If I was too unobtrusive about it half of his things might get left behind, inconveniencing his Mum and disappointing him. I didn't want to use up his valuable last few hours with us doing something that he was less than keen to do, being rather casual about his belongings at the best of times. I could have done it all for him and said nothing, as it had to involve me because of laundry considerations. But a lot of his stuff was books, toys and games I couldn't really be expected to know about let alone find! And I thought he was old enough to take responsibility for his belongings to some extent, and that he ought to. After deliberating about all these factors I decided to go for a happy medium and said I would start the job off by putting together the dull things like clothes, and whatever I could remember he had distributed in various places round the house, and then get him to find the rest. Then I'd sit down with him and we'd go through together what we might have forgotten. This is more or less what happened and it seemed to work quite well. I didn't get left feeling like his slave, he participated in taking some responsibility for his things as well as remembering some things I would have forgotten. The whole operation was fairly quick and lighthearted. The next morning Dan remarked that he'd appreciated not having spent the whole evening on it, and between us only a few things got left behind! It seems I pitched it right that time despite my doubts.

Helping everyone get on together

Approach your step-children's visits just as you would if you were having any other of your children's friends to stay, and expect to be advised of any details such as health or timetable factors or other practical things. You'll be keen not to have them feel like strangers with their Dad or 'left out' now that he has a new family. Dad may be happy to let you take over the traditional mothering aspects of family life, especially if you've got your own children and are therefore already doing this. This is OK providing you and he have talked about this and you think they're ready to accept this from you. You may find these things get left to you anyway. Women tend to be more perceptive about the day-to-day details of life with children and you have a useful contribution to make in helping his children to feel at home. Try to involve them in some family decision making with everybody, perhaps about an outing or activity, and give them some responsibilities. Show interest in their schooling, friends and hobbies and invite them to get involved in your activities. There are probably some new activities and interests you can attract them into gradually, which will show them that you have some of your own special qualities to offer. Allow them a reasonable amount of privacy and make sure they give you some too.

If you're planning to have more children together, try to involve the ones you already have in your happiness about the expected event, but in a fairly low-key way. Don't worry about his children feeling replaced by any you have – this won't happen if you go on making sure everyone feels as important to all their parents (and step-parents) as they've always done. Give them some responsibilities for the baby so they can feel involved. Try to make sure family life continues pretty much as usual while his children are with you after the baby arrives. You'll be extra busy of course, but try not to seem too preoccupied with baby when his children are visiting.

His children and yours will be quick to notice if more than one set of limits and privileges creeps in. Try to avoid overreacting to what may seem like unnecessary comparisons or competitiveness. Sticking to the way you deal with your children will usually be best in the long run.

While the times when his children are with you will seem like special occasions and a time for treats and extra fun, don't feel you've always got to lay on something special or make special allowances. Mucking in with what you're doing and being a natural part of how you lead your life when they're not with you (with all its ups and downs, treats and routines) will be what they need to help make their time with you feel low-key, easy-going and valuable. It will also prevent your children feeling that his always seem to get treated extra specially.

Depending on the ages of all the children, as well as their temperaments of course, they won't necessarily become instant friends themselves. But they'll probably get on all right and this'll certainly make it easier for you. Beware of letting your own very natural hopes that your children and his will become good friends create expectations for this to happen too quickly. To begin with they'll probably think it's great fun to have new playmates if they're fairly similar in age, but in time they may find some tensions and rivalries intruding. Allow opportunities for his children to do things exclusively with their Dad when you can, without this being too contrived and unnatural. If your combined children's ages cover a wide range, you will of course want to be doing different things in different combinations anyway.

Communication is vital

Talking things over with your partner is essential for the success of any relationship, and is extra important the second time around (see Chapter 5). Don't forget to look after the relationship you have with your partner, which is after all the whole reason why you all came together. With all the extras of your ready-made family, the primary relationship can get neglected. It already has a handicap in that you've not had time on your own to build your relationship before you started a family. *If your relationship with the children's father is good and it flourishes, you're much more likely to have a successful step-family.*

Discuss the children regularly with their father so he can understand your position and so you can agree on and update your policies and practices with the children. For your own sanity and your children's good training – yours *and* his – you have to have the confidence to issue rules and set limits without worrying that you'll be resented for it, or rejected by a child who isn't 'yours'. Everyone in your ready-made family is really much more likely to respect you for the strength of character you can show, and children will feel secure in your company, even though at times they may appear to want to challenge everything you say or do. You don't have to be like your step-child's 'real' Mum: you need to be you. And if you're consistent, they won't be confused by being part of two households – the odds are they'll benefit by regular exposure to more than one kind of parent. If resentment over an issue builds up, have a family conference about it, including everybody, after you've discussed it with their father. Try and be reasonably honest about your feelings and encourage everybody else to be. Don't make the mistake of thinking you can't bring things up that are on your mind because you should be coping. Many step-parents say they didn't really do much thinking or planning about how their new family would work out. They just assumed that once they'd made the decision about their new love, things would probably take care of themselves. It's only later that they find all these new extra relationships are harder than they'd realised, and there are no clear guidelines about how everybody is supposed to operate, as there seem to be in families where everyone is related biologically and lives together all or most of the time. What you should be aiming for in the way you approach your family is to take part in talking issues over, so they are out in the open, acknowledged and taken into account, without being made too much of. If family tensions can be aired this way from time to time, then everyone will be freer to get on with the business of family life in a positive and easy-going way. *Being a successful step-parent is not about wearing kid gloves all the time, but about having insight into family relationships and anticipating all the different influences of blood ties, marriage bonds and past histories.*

How to feel more relaxed about it

An unfortunate legacy of the 'wicked step-mother' stereotype is that it can make you too anxious to be liked too soon, so as to counteract those negative associations. Knowing deep down that these children are the product of your lover's time with another woman can make you very anxious to excel in your new role, and rather sensitive to their reactions to you and how you compare in their minds with her. This feeling is most likely mainly in your head, except during the early stages of your acquaintance when comparing you with their Mum is part of them 'sizing you up'. Children do have enough room in their lives for more than one female caretaker or mother figure without comparisons or confusion, although it may take time for them to accept you. Their mother has a permanent relationship with your partner because of them, and you have to accept this fully if it's all going to work out well.

You may sometimes find it hard that accepting her also means accepting a continual drain on your family finances because you're paying her a contribution to the upkeep of the children. This is part of what you took on when you made your commitment to your partner, so acknowledge that some aspects of this arrangement grate on you a bit. Financial responsibility is an important part of shared parenting, so you must accept it regardless of whether, for example, you think she's pulling her weight financially or not.

One of the dangers of worrying too much about what line to take with the children is overreacting, imagining things in their words and actions that aren't really there. We've seen in Chapter 4 how this can affect fathers who feel cut off from their children. When you're keen to be a successful step-mother and help your mixed family be happy and well-adjusted despite a divorce in the background, you can find yourself worrying unnecessarily about things children say and do. An awful lot of the things step-parents worry about and attribute to the children's blended family situation are things that happen all the time in any family, where the parents quite readily accept them as part of growing up and just get on with managing them as best they can. Children aren't necessarily permanently affected in undesirable ways by their parents having divorced or by having to cope with a step-mother and step-siblings. *Anyway, quite a lot of what young children do and say is really momentary and random, and doesn't signify an ongoing attitude or feeling about people or relationships.*

Being keen to see my step-son get on well with our own small children (he hadn't been to stay for a while), I was allowing a noisy and joyful game of tag and pleased at their being involved together having fun. But in the end because of the noise level and risk of injury I called an end to it.

My step-son rushed to his room and shut the door. Worried that he was upset at my stopping the game, I called out that I wasn't cross. He cheerily replied, 'It's OK, I know you're not.' In the typical fast pace of children, he'd just hurried off to another game of his own, leaving me worrying about having been a killjoy and a fussy step-mother, when in fact he hadn't given my restriction a moment's thought!

Be prepared to discover that you aren't getting the consideration, closeness and warmth that you may feel you deserve from children, when you're their part-time step-parent. You may feel it's all give and no take, and wonder whether it's all worth it, this one-sided relationship. Try not to give in to these feelings and 'switch off' from them. It really will be worth it in the end, and there won't be another chance to go back on these years. With each visit you're building the foundation of relationships that will go on for all your lifetimes.

You may miss the intimate trust and close communication you have with your own children, and you may be very aware of the differences between 'his' and 'yours'. Don't feel guilty about this, they *are* different, and what's more you can't be expected to necessarily like them just because you like their father, although you probably will (most of the time, anyway!). If you sometimes feel they really aren't all that likeable, don't worry, just make sure you try to accept and respect them. Don't 'give up' on them because you feel the way they are reflects deficiencies you see in their mother's approach to their upbringing – they need you to be accepting, not rejecting.

If at times you find you resent his children, don't forget that being an occasional father has its frustrating and sad moments and your partner needs all the support he can get from you in his restricted parenting role. Even though you may sometimes feel they interfere with your own relationship with their father (like John's wife did, above), his children need him to be part of their lives, regardless of whether their mother has remarried. Their continued relationship with him is helping them adjust to their parents having split up. You are an important part of their lives now and they stand to gain a lot from you too as a part-time parent, and as the person who is partner to their father.

Seeing rewards for your efforts

As you get to know the children better, you'll probably find you become more confident with them and able to share the responsibility for them more equally with their father. You'll be able to stop thinking they're comparing you all the time with their mother, and you'll become more relaxed in your role as their part-time caretaker. You'll find they come to you for the things they know mothers provide, which will give you opportunities to develop your special ways of relating to them.

You can come to really enjoy some things about the different tie you have with step-children. You can be more detached about their faults, for instance, not feeling yourself responsible for them or for trying to fix them up. This detachment may enable you to be more accepting of them, more able to appreciate their achievements than a natural parent sometimes can, giving them a different kind of respect for you. You may be free of the high expectations that biological parents often have of their children, and they will enjoy the freedom this makes them feel with you. You don't have to worry about their moral training the way their parent does either. You can maybe have an occasional special day with step-children, giving them a treat without worrying about spoiling them, enjoying the same pleasure that a grandparent does with grandchildren.

You can't expect to get as much back emotionally for what you give a child when you're only a part-time step-parent. In that respect (and of course, in many other ways too) it's quite a different relationship from the one you have with your own children. I sometimes want to talk to my step-son about things I can't really expect him to be interested in sharing with someone who isn't his usual confidante. I loved my step-son from the beginning because he is my husband's son, but it's rather a one-way relationship. I feel I put quite a lot into my relationship with him, but I try to remind myself that if I expect too much back from him, I'm really asking him to treat me just like he does his Mum, and he probably doesn't need that. There can be great moments, for me as well as him, though. When sometimes my 'part-time child' calls me 'Mum' by mistake, I get a wonderful warm feeling inside that I must be doing alright and he must be fairly relaxed about it all, if I sometimes feel like a Mum to him.

In time you can come to have a unique kind of relationship with your step-children. While you may feel that there are complications and frustrations to be overcome at first, there is great potential for a close guiding friendship to develop that is enriching both emotionally and educationally, even if you don't see your step-children all that often. *You can be a unique and valuable part of their lives precisely because you are not their 'real' parent, certainly not in spite of it!*

7

Maintaining Authority

Staying in charge of your family as its head, whether you're parenting on your own or in partnership is crucial to successful family life. But whatever the ages of your children and your own family circumstances, there are probably times when you can remember feeling a sense of powerlessness as a parent.

It isn't just the stresses of separation and family change, single parenting, financial worries and fatigue that contribute to feeling disorganised and lacking in authority though, so don't think it's just your 'situation'. These things just mean that it's even more important than ever to feel in charge, because they make it harder to hang onto your authority and to foresee the effects of losing it.

So it's more than just the bad patch you're going through, it's a subtle combination of significant changes in how we approach parenting and family life nowadays, which doesn't make it any easier to feel in charge. You've probably noticed parents in your circle of friends complaining about what sounds like a loss of their own authority. They can't get their children to do what they expect of them, don't get much respect from them, and tend to blame other people and events for their own dissatisfactions. Infuriating and unmanageable teenagers for instance, have almost become the expected thing.

When you are regularly frustrated by people in your family, you aren't in charge yourself, you feel governed by your circumstances, you are without power.

Whatever happened to parental authority?

You don't have to struggle through a sociology text to realise what's contributed to the undermining of authority within families. After two world wars Western cultures, threatened by an authoritarian takeover, reacted strongly with a new liberalism. And at a time when Freud and the ego psychologists were telling us that parenting practices had a permanent effect on personality development, and freedom to express creative individuality must be encouraged, people were ready to reject the control and strictness associated with so-called 'Victorian' parenting styles. This, combined with post-war affirmation of the importance (to population growth) of family life and specifically full-time motherhood, resulted in a very child-centred, 'free range' approach to parenting. Children, so the theory went, should grow up unrestricted in pursuit of their own individuality, which of course is often at the expense of a parent's own needs and the family's collective interests.

Added to these trends are other significant changes of the last couple of decades. Economic forces mean that people move further afield to get employment, cutting themselves off from the support and solidarity of extended families. Health and welfare services and subsidies have become available, tending to substitute people's ordinary sense of responsibility for the well-being of the family. An increasingly materialist culture and higher standards of living mean that definitions of personal success have tended more and more to be in terms of material wealth than the production of successful children, further eroding the perceived worth of parenting. Feminism has suggested that marriage, parenting and family life place unfair limits on what women can otherwise achieve, almost as if other achievements might be somehow more worthwhile! The fashion industry undermines motherhood by deliberately promoting a supposedly ideal female image, pencil-thin, unfertile-looking and consuming huge amounts of time and money on presentation. This 'ideal' could not be more ill-fitted for the practicalities of life like

112

running for a bus or scooping up a toddler; she is in fact the very opposite of everything associated with pregnancy and motherhood. So many modern women find themselves feeling ambivalent about parenting, creating tensions in the way they perform as mothers (and step-mothers), confusing fathers because of their changed expections about shared parenting, and finding themselves saying to people, 'I'm only a housewife!'

Authority is so important to successful families that it's worth reminding yourself of the fact again and again, to help you hang on to 'being in charge'. In your extra-complicated family circumstances it's even more important to stay one step ahead, but even harder to do so.

Why have rules at all?

The family is a group whose main purpose is the production, protection and training of new people who can form new groups, ensuring continuity. Any group has to have rules and standards for behaviour if it is to achieve anything, otherwise self-interested chaos results. For these rules to work the group must have a system for implementing them. Someone must have a delegation to 'keep order', ensure rules are respected and inflict penalties. So there has to be an authority.

Your children begin as novice members of your group, with you in charge of their training for life. The family is the training ground for most of what we must learn for life outside the family. Constructive learning can't happen without guidance, and guidance requires authority and direction. What we learn inside our family about order and authority teaches us how social order in the world outside depends on sustaining a hierarchy of authority which everyone contributes to in some way. You have to help your children fit in 'out there', so they have to learn about rules and systems from you.

Authoritative parenting

What exactly is this kind of authority we're saying is so much under pressure from modern attitudes as well as separation circumstances? It is being (and feeling) in charge of yourself and your emotional life; accurately anticipating the feelings and reactions of others and taking them into account in the way you operate; having the confidence to set firm and consistent limits as well as encourage both creative and emotional expression, especially with children; feeling satisfied (rather than frustrated) most of the time with your family and all its relationships; earning and expecting respect, and so receiving it.

To be successful at anything you have to feel good about what you're doing. As a parent you need to feel positive about your role, although it's harder to excel at a job you don't feel admired for or get paid for, and sometimes don't even feel appreciated for within the family. You need physical and emotional strength to cope with the growing and changing needs of children, especially in step-families. *Feeling good about it comes from knowing inside yourself and never forgetting how very important parenting is and realising that you can't go back and have another go at it – all of what you do in families counts.* When you think about it, we can influence the world through what we transmit to our children over generations, and have a much more lasting impact on it than we can through most of the other things we do and may feel more admired for. If you can be positive and confident you'll stay in control because you won't let your circumstances get the better of you.

What do we want from our children?

We all want our children to be givers as well as takers, and to show respect and obedience most of the time. This only comes from assertive, authoritative, powerful parenting. You need to give firm clear leadership and ask for polite respect in return. We can only accept our children (and they us) once we accept ourselves, which means thinking and acting as if we do, setting limits on our children's demands of us and not putting our own needs or theirs first all of the time.

The two of you as foundation members of your family group must have trust and interdependence as a unit. Parent-child relationships must be two-way; just being given to is never enough to satisfy children. Once past infancy, a child can start to learn the beginnings of giving as well as taking, of sharing and of waiting. Then with warmth and consistency, parental authority can be skilfully exercised and these beginnings progressively built upon.

We want our children to weather the reorganisation of their 'group' after its leaders gave up trying to get on together. Separating presents real challenges to parental authority and to getting what you want for and from your children. It can make you let children have too much choice, too much power, because you aren't in control of things as much as you need to be, and maybe unaware of what this does in families, and especially families in which there are children who are also regularly part of another family.

What happens when authority gets lost

When you're still recovering emotionally from your separation, the business of the children's contact with both their parents is especially vulnerable. If your feelings about the person they're meant to go on loving are a mixture of love, anger, exasperation, downright hate sometimes, and certainly lost trust, there's a very great danger that you'll lose the personal strength you very much need to help this relationship establish itself on a new basis. It's a tall order to have to foster this bond when your personal feelings are so involved. However much parents believe in the importance of it, they very commonly let their own feelings influence the arrangements in unhelpful ways. You'll find yourself suspecting his motives for wanting to see the children if he's just left you (remember Anne in Chapter 1?), maybe apprehensive before he calls to pick them up, even a little bit threatened yourself by the idea of your kids loving and wanting this man. Mothers often say, 'I think it's terribly important that the kids go on spending time with Dad, they can go to his place whenever they want to, it's fine by me, I've no objections.' The danger here is that this reflects a passive attitude about the children's relationship with Dad. It contains the suggestion that there could be an objection, that permission is necessary, which once obtained is all that's needed for the relationship to happen. This leaves too much choice with the children, who will find it hard to take the initiative themselves if there's the slightest hint of ill feeling or anxiety coming from Mum about Dad. If they don't feel you utterly approve of them leaving you to see him, if Dad coming to collect them makes you up-tight, they'll sense it. If you don't take charge and actively get the visiting going by lightheartedly insisting that what you've arranged happens, then you may accidentally convey your own doubts about it. And in the early stages, they may not fully appreciate what seeing Dad this way is going to be like and how important it's going to be in the longer term, and just need you to give them that extra nudge. They may opt to do what seems easier for them, which may be to not bother about Dad at all for the moment.

All these things threaten children's freedom to enjoy important relationships. We talked about how to handle children seeming reluctant about visiting in Chapter 4. Of course many of these things apply to Dad and his approach to the children's relationship with Mum. You absolutely must be one step ahead of your own feelings on this one and carry out your real responsibility towards them in a lighthearted and easy-going way, despite your hurt. This is *really* being in charge.

Part-time parents have to accept that they aren't going to be able to have as much authority or say about their children as they used to or would like to. For some fathers this is very hard to accept. All the differences between Mum and Dad about approaches to the children are exaggerated and you're worried about the children's characters suffering, perhaps because you think she's too soft on a lot of issues. Beware of undermining their respect for her by trying to assert your standards too forcefully over things which really are mainly her responsibility now you're separated. But continue to maintain your standards when they're with you without drawing attention to the fact that they're different. If she's remarried you have to accept that the male adult they are with most of the time, and who they know is important to Mum, is bound to have to have a lot of say over the day-to-day concerns of your children. This can be hard but you must accept this, realising that it needn't necessarily threaten your authority over the children (see also Chapter 4). Their relationship with you is a different one and how it works in terms of respect and order is largely up to you.

My step-son Adam has been disobedient lately. It makes me mad when he's rude to his Mum, and I want to have some say with him, and order and respect in the house, even though they see their real Dad a lot. The other day there was an argument about a TV programme which ended up with him being really rude, so I stepped in and decided he should lose his pocket money for a fortnight as well as apologise. His Mum and I agreed we'd stick to this as a punishment, but it didn't carry much weight because the next weekend he came back with some extra money he'd got from his Dad. I don't know for sure whether he told his Dad why he was short of money, but if he did it wouldn't surprise me if it made his father more inclined to bail him out, just to interfere with our authority. It certainly makes it difficult to keep in charge, and I feel helpless when this sort of thing happens. And even if Adam didn't tell him why he was short, it would've been easy for him to play 'poor me' and get what he wanted out of his Dad who seems to like spoiling him.

You'll probably carry with you for a long time a niggling concern about the effect your separation is having on the children, what it might have been like had things worked out better, what you should be doing differently to make it better for them. These are pretty normal feelings and they are an admirable reflection of your commitment to putting the children first. Your confidence in yourself will probably be a bit knocked, as anybody's is after a personal failure. Too much guilt or self-pity won't help though, and will tend to make you blame problems on the situation, problems that in happier times you would've taken in your stride as part of parenting. It's also likely to undermine your ability to parent assertively. You'll worry about whether you're getting it right and end up being a bit too flexible and inconsistent or tentative, when you're not sure what's the best policy. Relations between your children's two families may suffer. You're ready to take too much of the responsibility for how everyone is getting on together (you inflicted a divorce on them so you must be responsible), which paves the way for them to place the blame on you for everything that doesn't go their way. In effect they'll have started to control you rather than the reverse. The result may be insecure, defiant or uncooperative children, not to mention a frustrated and irritable parent!

A great many parents have a natural inclination to make concessions because of the difficult situation they know their children are in. Even without any guilt or anxiety operating (see above), it's part of the many parental instincts we have, to show sympathy and compassion and make allowances when our children are having to cope with extra things in their lives. This is fine of course, but there are ways of doing this which won't risk undermining your position as their caretaker or make it difficult to pull in the reins when you've all recovered from the emotional upheaval and adjusted to your new lives. It's even more important than usual for you to assert your authority firmly because rules make children feel reassured. Their lives have changed because of what's happened and they'll be feeling insecure. They may feel awkward about visiting Dad until they know the rules, so don't make the mistake of not issuing any – you can do it in a firm but kindly, even humorous way. You'll do them a favour if you show that this important aspect of living together in a family hasn't got lost (see also Chapter 4). They'll be reassured to feel that you're strong, reliable and in charge, not 'all over the place' emotionally. You haven't 'given up' on being a parent because you can't see how you can be an adequate one any more, and a 'take it as it comes' approach seems easier.

A management responsibility which is shared won't work without good communication; neither will your management of parenting. You now have a major drawback to communication with your co-manager in the form of emotional estrangement, and what's more your responsibilities are exercised in two separate places. A manager's nightmare! Your charges are in a perfect position to play one of their managers off against the other and manipulate you, if you don't keep in touch about them at least minimally, as the story of Adam (above) shows.

As we saw in Chapter 5, there are grey boundaries in step-families over who's responsible for what. This may mean people don't know what's expected of them and end up making decisions and choices themselves, or get more than one set of rules and standards and end up uncertain or manipulative. It's easy to see how a natural parent's desire to make concessions (see above) and the sometimes varying standards in a step-family can combine to create confusion and annoyances.

Age differences can cause authority problems. When a father marries someone not that much older than his oldest child, his relationship with his child, especially if she's a girl, may suffer. We talked about generational confusion in Chapter 5. It can have a profound effect on children's willingness to cooperate and their respect for your authority.

When I was 24 I got married to Jim, who had a fourteen-year-old daughter. I really had no idea how to relate to her to start with. I think I naively thought that Jim would always be there when permission or decisions or organisation was needed, and that I wouldn't need to be very involved. I soon found that circumstances were always putting me in a parent role about things like spending money, staying out late, homework, and it was really awkward. I could see she resented me because of my age and I guess I can't blame her for this. Jim and I were both afraid she might opt out of seeing her Dad altogether because of me. We settled into a fairly workable relationship gradually. I tried to make her feel I wasn't giving her permission for things, but rather passing on my reasons for having an opinion one way or the other, recommending a particular angle, referring the matter to her father for a policy on the issue. I think it's impossible to have parental authority in this situation. You have to aim for something more realistic, a sisterly kind of relationship like a good friend. But the step-daughter has to respect you as their father's wife too. They can respect you as a friend and adviser if you make an effort to listen to their concerns and be a helper. Once I realised that she was probably jealous of the attention I got from her father, we made a point of toning down how much cuddling and private talking we did in front of her. Jim took her aside and had a bit of a talk with her about the different ways in which he loved both of us (he should have done this right at the start I think).

How to stay in charge

Several points we've made in other chapters also fit importantly into a discussion about being one step ahead in your family. Here's what you should be doing to try and get there (or stay there!):

- Do what you think is right at the time without seeming to hesitate too much. Be decisive. If you're left in doubt about whether you dealt with something the best way, discuss it later with your partner and form a policy. Don't give in half the time because you're worn out, fragile or can't be bothered. It'll be much harder to get cooperation when you do have to insist. This is particularly important with younger children because you can't successfully appeal to a sense of logic and reason about flexibility and exceptions to rules (but luckily their memories are short!). You'll be much more confident if you have a partner whose backing you know you have and with whom you can combine ideas regularly. Then the children won't be able to go and get what they want from your partner after not getting it from you.

- Keep your children informed about what's happening in the family that concerns them, especially about arrangements between households. This begins at separation time (see Chapters 3 and 5). Remember, do this in a way that takes into account their views and feelings, but doesn't make them feel they've decided the issue themselves, or that decisions can necessarily be altered by them. Children need to feel in touch and involved rather than left out and 'parcelled around'.

- Try to make use of the personal security and confidence you have (yes, it's there somewhere!) to support and encourage your child's time with the other parent, not only in your outlook but also in your words and actions. Remember the benefits of the obvious when trying to get your children to do something you've planned for them that they feel reluctant or uncertain about. Sometimes when you get exasperated with your children not cooperating, you forget to show patience and acceptance of their feelings. Take them aside, give them a hug and say something encouraging like, 'You're sure to find you have fun, sometimes people hesitate and then miss out on happy things, we all have to do things we think we'd rather not sometimes, so off you go, I'm happy for you, etc.', pitched for their age of course. This is much more powerful

121

parenting than showing exasperated insistence, and can be very usefully applied to children's passage between estranged parents.

- It's surprising how often children feel in the dark about things, and they can't feel secure or comply if they don't know what's expected of them. Part-time parents, as we saw, may especially need to remember this. The children may forget and need to be reminded between visits about how you do things here. Deliver re-issues at the beginning of a visit and you'll be one step ahead and probably prevent one or two disagreements. If they know where they stand, you'll need to pull them into line less often. Remember, don't be afraid to give reminders or make new rules for fear of sounding like a nag. You may be worried about your child rejecting your authority, and even you, when you feel your relationship with them is a bit tenuous. But in the long run they'll respect your needs and take them into account, if they know what the limits are. These are for you to set.

- You and your partner must be the basis of authority in your family. Children in families headed by a couple who present a united front are usually more secure and respectful. In step-families in particular it's vital that the couple is a unit which can't be undermined by children playing power games. Parents must stick together to stop divisive behaviour even if they feel differently about it; they must see each other's position and be supportive of it. To create this unity you and your partner need to look regularly at the input and examples you give the family, and at how many of your rules aren't all that important and you could be more flexible about. You must yourselves live up to the behaviour you demand, to sustain your children's respect. Parents are the most important models of behaviour and standards that children have.

My wife and I had agreed to divorce but we remained in the same house for a while. There were a number of reasons for doing this which made sense at the time. Because my wife and I were not talking to each other at all while Adrian was carrying on as usual with us both, he was in a perfect position to work things very much to his advantage. Money had been a sore point since communication had broken down with Jean, and Adrian would say to me something such as, 'Mum says I can't have new Hi-tops because she hasn't the money for my clothes because you aren't giving her enough.' Of course I knew exactly how much she had and that she was out and about socialising, so no wonder there was none left for important things . . . Jean was obviously trying to make a point to me through our son, but suddenly I saw the scope that Adrian had to play one of us off against the other because he knew we weren't talking, and because obviously I couldn't say anything to him which put his mother in a bad light. So I decided the best way to stay ahead on this issue would be to pre-empt things by lightheartedly saying to Adrian what a great position he was in in some ways with the two of us not talking and what scope there was for getting the best out of both of us. I figured that if I could show I was one step ahead in appreciating his position, then he'd be much less likely to manipulate mine. So far I think it's worked and I feel my showing I appreciated his position sort of helped in a way.

- Don't assert your authority by shouting, loud scolding or issuing threats. When you resort to this method of trying to get cooperation you give up your position as a mature and moral guide, because the confrontation tends to degenerate into a contest over who can shout the loudest and you become like an angry child yourself. You'll probably feel ashamed at what you sound like. Threats are demeaning or frightening, and children usually learn pretty quickly that you wouldn't really carry out what you're threatening anyway. Children can be very irritating at the best of times; inexperienced and impulsive, exuberant, impatient, self-centred, tiring, noisy, time-consuming and lots more! So of course most of us find we 'blow our stack' sometimes, especially if we're under pressure. This doesn't set a very good example. It can help to refer to the exchange as soon as everybody has recovered, explain how cross you were and that you had good reason to be, but that you regret the outburst. With young children, who have short memories, it can help to refer back to an incident from the day before, say, and remind them of what they did, why it was wrong and why they were punished. We all raise our voices as a reflex sometimes, in order to have impact. Listen out for how often you actually do this and what effect it has. You may decide a rethink is warranted.

- Assert your authority by giving warnings, especially to young children, about what's got to happen soon. They don't like being packaged or stopping what they're doing, and are likely to resist when you spring things on them 'without notice'. Their sense of time is quite different to yours and it's easy to forget to explain things to children in our eagerness to get things done. Giving a 'five-minute gun' identifies with their sense of time and often effectively reduces protests. Getting ready to go back to Mum's or go over to Dad's, for example, is something you want to keep as hassle-free as possible. Use counting, for example: 'I'll count to ten and then you've got to pack up and go and clean your teeth'. This gives a child the chance to comply before you pull rank. Use diverting or redirecting tactics which will work when the problem is boredom. With young children who have short memories, distract their attention onto something interestingly different from whatever it is they won't stop doing.

- If you don't succeed in getting cooperation, or you must impose a punishment, use time-out for younger children. Send them to their room or somewhere on their own for a specified time and only let them come out if they're ready to cooperate or apologise. When everybody has calmed down, explain what they did wrong and why they had to be punished. This will help the lesson sink in and will avoid any misunderstanding they might have about the incident. Stick to this despite their protests and it'll work. For older children, punish by withholding privileges. Insist on an apology and don't give in.

- Each of you must, within reason, speak out about whatever annoys you. You can do this without making too big a deal about it, treating it as just as much a part of your character that you get annoyed by something as it is inconsiderate on the part of whoever does it. This way you're likely to gain respect because you're acknowledging some responsibility, making your views known without attacking anyone personally, and setting important and necessary limits in a reasonable way.

- Be willing to listen, take an interest in and accept other people's point of view, without necessarily agreeing with it. Be willing to take responsibility for your contribution to things (see above). This will help gain you respect. Time spent attending to children at their level, whether it's working, playing or just listening, earns their respect. Children generally want to cooperate with people they admire and respect.

- Don't, because you feel silly, cover up your frustration about something till you blow up at the last trivial straw. This can make one person bear the brunt of a whole lot of accumulated frustrations they had little to do with, which can be confusing and hurtful.

- Encourage children to help you with household tasks, even from an early age. Don't stop them volunteering to 'help' at age two because you know they're going to be more of a hindrance and the job will take ages. This is a tall order for busy parents and you'll wonder whether it's a reasonable goal. But you can't very well expect them to be willingly helpful later just because they're old enough to be really useful, if they haven't learnt about doing things with and for other people and are oblivious of what goes into keeping a house running. Small children love to help if they're allowed to and it's a chance for some pleasurable and humorous sharing as well as getting things done while being together. It may also help prevent you feeling like everyone's slave later on when you can't get their cooperation with the routine aspects of living together however hard you try.

- Try to be detached and distance yourself from what goes on in the other household. You mightn't like or approve of all you hear and suspect about it. But since you can't do much (if anything) about it, there's no point in being over-curious about the other part of your children's life. You'll feel more in control of your circumstances if you can cultivate this detachment because you will no longer be letting yourself get affected by things you have no control over. Just show interest in and support for what goes on over there, and avoid any temptation you may have to do anything – like phone too often – that might be seen as interfering. The spin-off with cultivating detachment (not disinterest) is that you will contribute to allowing your children the freedom to be part of two families without their having to worry about what this does to you (see also Chapter 2).

- At all costs don't involve your children in the potentially in-criminating business of your divorce, like property, maintenance, infidelities, etc., unless they're really mature enough to have a trusting heart-to-heart about relationship breakups in general and they seem to want to know more. We talked about the hazards of involving children in 'setting the record straight' and how it apportions blame in Chapter 2. And once children know something about what's going on in these adult matters, you lose control over them yourself because you don't know what the children may be saying to others or thinking to themselves, and they probably don't really understand it all anyway. They certainly shouldn't feel they have a part to play in resolving disagreements between their own parents!

- There's sometimes a very delicate situation that can test your position to the limits, which we talked about from the position of part-time parents in Chapter 4. It's handling with detached foresight the remarks children make occasionally, even long after your separation, about where they'd like to live. They may only be making a statement about something they feel bad about that happened 'over there' last week. But there are lots of reasons why it's so delicate. For part-time parents, children saying, 'I'd like to live with you, Dad', is a powerful expression of love for him that is wonderfully gratifying for an estranged parent to hear. He may feel that all the reservations he's ever had about Mum and her household have at last been independently perceived by his children, in spite of having backed the arrangements to the hilt all this time. But the children may just be saying that they like being with their Dad. And for Mum, it's not only threatening for her to wonder about her relationship with her children and how much she's caused them to pine for Dad, but also it brings up all sorts of worries about whether anything should be done about what the children seem to be feeling. This reflects a dangerous competitiveness resulting from your marital differences about who has most to offer your children and doubts about who they're going to turn out most like. This situation is one of the most important issues over which parental authority and cooperation is necessary. It can arouse such strong feelings between parent and child. It is the stuff that legal battles for custody are made of. But you will be able to see that, despite these strong feelings, you must appreciate your children's point of view, react to that and not to your own feelings. Otherwise you will risk giving your children a burden of choice between their two parents that is heart-rending as well as confusing. If you say things like, 'Well, you can if you still want to when you're older', or 'Talk to your mother and see if she'll let you', or 'Yes, I really want you to', or 'Sure, you can go and stay at Dad's whenever you want to', you reinforce the notion that the children have a choice about major changes in arrangements; a choice in favour of one parent at the expense of the other. This should never be a choice for a child to make. Hold on to your authority over your children's bonds, welcome the remark for what it says about the strength of your children's feelings for one of their parents. Take a long, hard, honest look at how things are really going before talking things over with your 'ex' and your present partner. Only then should you even think to discuss whether anything should be substantially changed.

Golden rules for staying in charge

These five rules will help you maintain your authority:

1. Work out what you want; set the scene early on for being one step ahead whenever you can, by working out carefully what you want for your family, especially your children, given your circumstances.
2. Consider your children's needs; take into account their ages, experience, likely point of view, their individual characters including their sensitive areas.
3. Decide what adult attitudes must be taken into account; combine this with an honest appraisal of any emotional blockages or significant attitudes on your part, and on the part of significant other adults in your children's lives.
4. Work out how your family is going to work: make a plan of how you're going to handle reorganised family life in a way that makes sense to you, so you can do it with confidence.
5. Proceed with confidence: get on with life, asserting yourself with warmth, firmness, enthusiasm, good humour, a willingness to listen and even compromise sometimes. You'll get there.

8

Understanding Children and Divorce

So far we've talked throughout about knowing and respecting how family goings-on feel for children. Satisfying and productive relationships which help children thrive depend on there being mutual understanding and respect. Here we're going to look further into the effects of breakups on children so you know what to look out for and what to do about it, and get a better understanding of what they experience. Then we'll look at ways of relating effectively to children, especially over divorce topics.

Children and breakups

Children are affected emotionally in some way by their parents' separation, but usually only for a time of transition while everybody adjusts to the loss of the original family and gets used to new relationships. We saw in Chapter 2 how it's the family circumstances surrounding a divorce (extreme conflict, violence, sudden desertions, etc.) that can affect children more than transiently, not the divorce itself. So if you're getting it even half right, you needn't worry too much about how your children will fare. You need only be one step ahead in anticipating how your children are going to cope so you can work out ways of making it easier. A certain amount of worry of course is useful because it keeps you watchful. But it's pointless worrying more than a little – you can't change the fact of your divorce so it makes far more sense to make the best of it, helping your children get some useful experience in managing life's hurdles through your support and guidance.

Having said this, you should bear in mind that how they react to your separation and adjust over subsequent years will depend on three main things: how sensibly you yourselves handled the breakup and ongoing relationships; their age and stage of development at the time your separation became known to them; their individual temperaments – whether they are the easy-going or anxious type by nature, for instance.

Children too young to understand what's going on commonly refuse to believe the separation is going to be permanent. We mentioned this earlier in relation to getting used to step-parents. Older children often bitterly resent it. However poor the relationship between parents, unless there are extreme circumstances of abuse in the family, children would prefer it if their parents stayed together, and many dream of a reconciliation and will even go to some lengths to scheme one. Even constantly quarrelling parents are better than separated ones as far as the children are concerned, it seems. This reflects the profound longing children often experience for both their parents to be available to them all the time, and sadness at the permanent separateness of their parents' two different worlds.

Children tend to take guilt on themselves about the separation. They are themselves the centre of their whole life and thinking, so therefore (so they feel) they must be the centre of their parents' world. It follows that all their own minor and major misdemeanours must therefore have been what culminated in their parents deciding to destroy the family.

Older children tend to be aligned with the same sex parent as a natural part of their identity development, and are usually angry with the other parent, who they feel should have 'done better', has failed, and let them down:

I was fifteen when my mother finally told my father he had to leave, because he had another relationship going. He was never around much anyway. We're a religious family, well Mum and my brother and I anyway, and what Dad's done is unforgiveable. I know it's made Mum bitter and angry, and she lets fly at him quite often when he comes round to see if he can pick up Jamie. They don't talk because Mum won't, and she can't stand the way he just calls round any old time to see Jamie, and I reckon he's got no right to interfere with our life after what he's done. I don't go out with him any more, you see I belong to a youth group which has a strong sense of family and loyalty so how can I accept my father? Jamie goes over to his place every weekend but never when his friend is there. I actually think Jamie wouldn't mind meeting her, but if Mum found out he had, she'd be furious because she thinks – and I agree with her – that we shouldn't have anything to do with this person. When Dad calls round I can see Jamie has a hard time deciding whether to agree to go off with Dad. He sort of wants to please Mum by not going but really feels he shouldn't say no, and wants to be with Dad. This happens almost every time. The other Monday Dad asked Mum if he could pick Jamie up after table tennis club and take him out to tea if he got him home by 8.30, as it was a week night. Mum said no, saying he'd be too tired because he has an early start on Mondays because of band practice before school. I could see Jamie was relieved when Dad didn't try to insist he went. Mum said later that she'd said no because she had a date that night and didn't want Dad calling round and causing tension when she was expecting her friend and getting ready to go out.

In this story, it's easy to see how a child's tendency to align themselves with their major caretaker, a natural result of their security being threatened by their parents' split, can be exaggerated. Parents often aren't aware (especially part-time parents) of why children appear to 'side' with a close parent, and think the other parent has been deliberately influencing the children, as the father thought in this story. It's easy to see how a child's needs for security can easily hamper the visiting relationship if both parents aren't being confident, trusting and cheerful about their rearranged family.

Even though for you your separation may have been years ago, it stays with your children as some kind of memory forever, and so it should. Their origins are an important part of their emerging identity. Children should be allowed and even encouraged to discuss and mourn the loss of family life as they knew it. If they were very young children when you separated, like Katy in Chapter 2, their past will very much be in terms of what they've been told happened, and they won't of course experience loss or need to mourn, although they can feel a longing for something they've never had. New partners must remind themselves to accept that the absent parent will always be there, in reality or in memory. No amount of reframing or wishful thinking will erase their part in the history of your new family. It's as basic as remembering you can change partners but not parents!

Could they be seriously troubled?

It's unlikely that your children will react to your being divorced in a seriously pathological way, so don't be too ready to attribute what you see of concern in them to their family circumstances. And don't blame yourself and the fact that your marriage didn't work. We've agreed this isn't fruitful.

It is likely that at some time or another you'll ask yourself whether what you observe in their behaviour is something you should be doing more about. More, that is, than being confident, cheery, low-key, reassuring, positive and patient. Most children will show some signs that they are feeling troubled by what's happening in their family. You need to know that things like clinging insecurity, silent withdrawal, anger manifested in aggression or tantrums, sadness, lack of self-confidence, deterioration in school performance, distractibility, unsettling dreams and sleep disturbances are all part of children's reactions to stress and change and as such are ways of coping with the situation. You may notice that they seem to have reverted to a stage of competence that you thought they had progressed from, like not wanting to leave your side, or wetting the bed. Almost all children experience some of these things to some degree from time to time as they develop and they don't usually last for long, so don't be alarmed or feel guilty. Neither of these reactions will help. Blaming it on something you think your partner should be doing differently won't help much either unless you can talk things over together really trustingly, in which case you'll probably be doing this anyway. After considering this, if you think there's cause for concern about how your children are coping with life, first discuss your observations with your current partner and confidant, your 'ex', the children's teachers, and see what your combined thoughts can do to shed light on whether you have a problem that you could all assist with. If this doesn't work then consider seeking expert help. A good counsellor may be able to help you talk more constructively with your 'ex', if you're having trouble doing this. Problems that seem as if they are something to do with separation events are usually best dealt with by consultation and discussion between parents and a counsellor rather than (and certainly before) singling out a child as having a problem requiring treatment. If a child's social, family or school life seems severely impaired over a considerable period of time then consider consulting a child-guidance professional. Keeping a diary of all that you have observed of concern will help them to help you with the problem.

Don't forget that the power to help make your children's lives more comfortable lies with you because of your close relationship with them, and because you can help them express themselves about their world by encouraging them to communicate about it.

Resilience and vulnerability

Reassure yourself by knowing that most children are pretty resilient, sometimes surprisingly so. It takes a fair amount of sustained stress to disadvantage a child permanently. Some children are by nature slower than others in developing a sense of security and self-confidence. They may be the anxious, shy type, or the boisterous, angry kind. Or they may be affected by a developmental handicap of some kind which affects their self-image in some way, making them more vulnerable. Different temperamental characteristics may mean certain children cope better than others with the stress of family disruptions, and some may need more support and nurturing. You may have, or know of children who just seem to instinctively sail through life, others who seem to be worriers.

By now you'll know that by being aware of things like the importance of self-esteem, a sense of security, love and freedom from conflict between loved caretakers, you can do an enormous amount to improve the quality of your children's lives, and probably everybody else's too. Be aware of one or two further soft spots that need taking into account, even with apparently resilient children:

• Only children may be more affected than others at separation time and in subsequent years. Care needs to be taken to ensure they are able to be the child they are and are not made to feel too much of a companion to the parent they mostly live with. This can mean they are having to provide support to a parent at the expense of their own emotional needs. Siblings can be a great source of comfort to each other, through knowing that feelings of guilt are spread and through talking things over together as 'companions in adversity'.

• Your oldest child might seem rather more affected than younger siblings. This happens because they tend to feel responsible for the younger ones and because they feel an obligation to take on a more senior role in the family, to take the place of their mostly-absent parent. They may also feel they are bearing the burden on behalf of the others for how visiting arrangements are working out; they've become a sort of go-between.

• Children are very sensitive to the feelings their parents are radiating about everyone in the family, and it may surprise you just how much they pick up of what you're trying to hide. They mightn't be able to make sense of it, but they can certainly feel it, and the 'vibes' they get can inhibit their own freedom of feeling, and guide their loyalties, especially with young children. Here a teenager describes how she saw her parents relating:

It wasn't that she actually said anything against my father. But she didn't have to in so many words, because her disapproval of him came through loud and clear in other ways for years. When he came to pick us up, he'd be trying hard to be cheery (I suppose it was easier for him because he was happy to see us, if not too thrilled to see her!), but Mum would go all solemn and a bit stiff, and always send one of us to answer the door. She'd hardly say anything to him, which if you think about it, was quite rude, and he'd be trying to be conversational and low-key for our benefit I suppose. It all ended up with everyone feeling awkward, and us dreading pickup and return times, although we were always dying to see him. Mum was trying to be civilised in her own way but sometimes she made us feel uncomfortable about enjoying our time with Dad. When we talked about him and things we'd done with him, you could see she was trying to be interested, but the way she said 'Oh, really?' always seemed a bit suspicious and disapproving. So we talked about him less and less of course. And when he phoned and she answered, just the way she came in and said, 'It's your father', had a sort of resigned weariness to it, which I'm sure she didn't intend, but it was there. We got used to this and I guess the way we coped with it was to switch off and ignore it.

At one time it was really getting to me and I couldn't get angry with Mum so I had a heart-to-heart with Dad about it. I reckon what he said was really wise, considering his position. He said she was probably finding things a bit hard, but that her heart was in the right place about us spending time with him so we'd just have to try and ignore it, because she probably wasn't meaning to make us feel uncomfortable.

- Younger children experiencing this would be most likely to feel influenced, out of great loyalty to Mum who, as major caretaker, is most essential to their daily security. They'd feel they couldn't refer to Dad freely or enthusiastically. Yet Dad makes them feel warm and communicative about Mum. So a wall between two parents is constructed and the two worlds kept separate to minimise the contradictions they feel between their two parents.

- Young children's quite natural needs for security may be such that they even will feign indifference or criticism of Dad in such circumstances so as to please Mum. It's not hard to see then how Mum could get quite the wrong idea about her children's feelings for their father and therefore their contact with him, when what she's seeing in her children stems from their relationship with her rather than with him. Children should be able to relate to both their parents without having to devise elaborate coping strategies to protect their relationships in this sort of way. Here again it's the continuity of relationships with both parents that's vulnerable, when misunderstandings like this are generated.

- Children, especially during the period from about age eight to their teenage years, are quite materialistic. If you are in a position to provide a lot of material attractions you may create a longing in a child for your sort of life in the belief that being with you is somehow better because of what you offer. This longing can also develop because life in one household seems to be more free and easy or leisure-focused than in the other. These differences don't matter, but letting a child feel they have a choice about their arrangements if they express their preferences is usually mistaken, because they have to be preferences about one parent over the other.

When I was twelve I went to live with my father after talking it over with Mum, who said it was OK if this was what I really wanted. I'm not very sporty and Mum jogs and eats healthy food. I thought it would be good to be able to eat as much ice cream and Coke as I liked! I'd get away from my sister who I didn't get on with very well and Dad works long hours so I'd be able to please myself a lot. After a while I started to resent Dad, who didn't seem to have time to take an interest in me, and I was often a bit bored and lonely. Now I really feel guilty that I hurt Mum's feelings badly by going to Dad's, it's two years ago now. Now I don't really think I want to live with either of them because I don't know where I'd fit in. I stay with Mum whenever Dad goes away. Last time I found my sister and I were getting on really well, too. But I'm doing pretty badly at school, and really feel my father let me down.

Tuning in to children

Some people just seem to have a knack with kids, naturally attracting their interest and respect. They're obviously really committed to and comfortable with their role as a parent. We're not all like this, and kids are constant and demanding. Being divorced you have a useful motive to improve the way you relate to kids, most importantly yours. We'd all like to have children classify us as 'neat', 'ace', 'excellent', 'OK' or whatever the current buzz-word for favoured adults is, wouldn't we? Here are some pointers:

- There's nothing like spending time just together, as far as they're concerned. Be willing to stop what you're doing entirely, get 'on the floor' with them, and give your undivided attention to them over something quite simple.

- Be prepared to really play with them. Join in as an equal not always as someone with superior knowledge and experience, even pretending you need them to show you how to do things. Be abandoned and spontaneous sometimes so you're momentarily laughable, forgetting about dignity for a while.

- Don't forget how, even in our 'hi-tech' age, our children can be entertained simply when they are getting all the attention of a valued caretaker. This often allows time for building real trusting communication into a relationship. Children see you're not always preoccupied with your own chores and interests, happy that they're out of the way and being amused. Showing you find them worth spending time with tells them you think they are important to you.

- Don't forget to explain things to children. They are inexperienced, and everything in their life has to be learnt at some stage. You may be looking for more than they are yet capable of. Show respect for their position, tell them what you expect of them, or you may get frustrated when they won't (perhaps because they can't) cooperate or they make a mess of things. Try to make them keen to try, and not be afraid of disappointing you. You're working on building a relationship which guides a child onwards to a continuing sense of achievement.

- When you must disapprove, discipline or demand obedience, make sure you try to do it in a way which doesn't convey disrespect or dislike for your child personally. When you're cross it's easy to say things like, 'You're so stupid' or 'How come Joanne can always find her shoes and you never can?' Avoid comparisons with other children, especially their siblings, or making over-generalisations about their behaviour which create expectations which will tend to be lived up to (Mum says I'm stupid, so I must be). Examine your language, and make sure your message says that it's their behaviour, not them, that's unacceptable. There are effective ways of using authority which are not demeaning or undermining (see Chapter 7). Look at how often you find yourself issuing restraints – can you cut out some of the negative content of your exchanges with kids? For example, younger children naturally dawdle, so are you leaving enough time to get them organised? Can you put out of sight at least some of the things you can't allow them to tinker with? Try not to get irritated and impatient so that they feel they regularly exasperate you.

- Parents often complain that their children don't seem able to amuse themselves independently. Children learn to do this from you and their teachers. They need to learn the joy of discovery and the value of perseverance. This is an important part of learning to be independent. Have plenty of ideas up your sleeve which you're willing to spend some time introducing them to. Involve them in 'helping' you with your hobbies and interests, and watch how much time you let them spend being entertained passively, e.g. watching television.

- Don't give young children too much choice about things in an effort to treat them with respect. They'd often rather not have to think too hard about what to have for breakfast, or what to wear, for example. And definitely don't give them a choice when you have a preference yourself which you intend to insist on. This happens surprisingly often without parents realising they're doing it. Listen to yourself.

• Children don't necessarily know what they think and feel about things (nor do a lot of adults, for that matter!), nor do they express themselves in an organised or consistent way all the time. A lot of what you hear will not seem very logical, because it's spontaneous, momentary and random. They often say things just for impact, to excite, provoke, disturb, annoy, express anger and to manipulate. Try not to let this sort of exuberance get to you personally so you feel you must be failing somewhere; a certain amount of it is normal. They're learning what they think and feel about themselves and the world, and about what limits will be set on their behaviour. You don't need to react literally to everything they say or do but you should definitely set limits on destructive, hurtful and rude talk unless they're very obviously play-acting. Children can't reliably distinguish between fantasy and reality until they're five or more, and once they can they go on using their imagination actively in play. We've talked about the importance of interpreting children's remarks for what they are under various headings – it's important.

Rob [eleven] was staying with us for school holidays and he'd been out for the day with our neighbour's ten-year-old. My children by my second marriage are a fair bit younger so they don't always do everything together when Rob's with us. On this occasion it amused me to hear Rob, just when he got home, immediately starting to chase his younger brother and sister round the house, playing a very exuberant hiding game, causing lots of noise. When I interrupted to ask Rob whether he'd had a good day, he came panting up to me saying, 'What a peaceful time I've had without these two disturbing the peace all day, they're so noisy and annoying, I had a much better time today than I would have with them around!' This amused us because he was very obviously enjoying stirring them up, happy to find them ready to play as soon as he walked in and so pleased to see him. I think he quite misses them between visits, and if he can't be with them all the time, he looks for the disadvantages of having small children around to make up for this. Or he might have wanted to pretend he wasn't interested in such junior games. Of course you never really know what's behind some of the things they come up with, and half the time I don't think kids really know themselves. A divorce in the past tends to make you want to think about what's behind what they do and say more than you would in an ordinary family.

- Children aren't naturally forthcoming once the moment has passed, they move on to the next event or feeling quickly. As a consequence they may appear unenthusiastic, even secretive. Don't insist that they discuss something with you, strike a balance between sounding interested but not pushy. They'll tell you as and when they want you to know.

We only see David every six months or so because of distance and although we don't get much chance to talk things over with his Mum it seems to have gone quite well over the years. He seems to keep his two worlds pretty separate though. We try to show interest in his news from home, and we get sent his school reports. The other day we were asking a few conversational questions about his school and how he saw his immediate future shaping up there, and he responded in a noticeably reluctant way. Not upset or anything, but his normal bright way of speaking changed and he started to say various things in a mumbling, not very coherent way. We have no real reason to think there's anything to be concerned about, and it was probably just that it's easier for him to handle the fact that he has two separate worlds with close links in both by keeping them separate in his mind most of the time. It was clear he didn't really want to talk about school much (after all he was on holiday!), perhaps because his school life is associated with everything about not being with us. We both (his step-mother and I) said to each other later how we'd noticed it, but didn't draw attention to it with David – we just started talking about something else. You just have to accept it's probably his way of coping. I don't think it's a good idea to appear to challenge the way children are, by talking about things to do with feelings about 'the situation' too often. But you find you make a mental note of observations like this one, and maybe have them in mind when you do have the opportunity for a heart-to-heart from time to time.

If parents can relate to their children in an open way which is respectful of the contributions of both to the family, past and present, then communication will be more likely to remain open and productive all round. This will mean that everyone's adjustment to changing circumstances, where belonging to two households and having multiple family relationships is going to be the norm, will be much, much easier.

Talking about fault, truth and feelings

This topic came up under the heading 'Fielding children's questions well' in Chapter 3, and from the point of view of part-time fathers in particular, in Chapter 4. What you all say to children over the years has a great bearing on how they perceive the reasons for why things are the way they are, and very many parents are concerned about talking to children about family matters, so we're going to look at this again here.

At separation time, children would like to be told something rather than nothing about what is happening, even if you don't know yourself for certain and it has to be rather open-ended. Despite your feelings, try and make the best out of the situation for them, by pointing out the pluses. For example, you can say how important it is for people who are troubled and uncertain about something to have a long and careful think about things; and that sometimes this works better when they do it on their own. You can say, perhaps together, that Daddy is going away, but that this doesn't mean he doesn't care for you any more, that he cares for Mummy still but in a different way that means they don't want to live together any more; that they will still see each other often; that the decision has been very carefully considered and that you know it won't be easy for them, etc. Leave out the bits which cast doubt on the integrity of a parent, like frequent infidelities, alcoholic rages, irresponsible expenditure, deceits, frank disrespect for one another, etc. If you can, try to sound as if you support and respect one another's view so that the children sense you can be a team. This sounds obvious and we've said it before, but despite yourself, you may find yourself doing and saying things on the spur of the moment that aren't all that team-like.

Later on, when the family is reorganised and the children know that both Mum and Dad are still available to them but on a new basis, they'll want to ask questions from time to time. You may find yourself uncertain about how best to answer them. It's important that they feel they can refer to what happened between you, that it's not a taboo subject because they sense you're reluctant to discuss it. They may decide that what you aren't telling them must be something really awful if it has to be secret. Keep your answers to their questions simple but sufficient to satisfy their curiosity. Don't forget there are certain things children can't be expected to understand because they are very adult or complex, such as the notion of romantic love, that not loving someone any more doesn't mean you hate them. Don't be tempted to volunteer too much in the way of explanations or announcements. Young

children especially cannot begin to understand the affairs of adults
and you will risk making them confused and anxious if you try
too hard to have them know what happened (see Chapter 2 on
setting the record straight).

I found it very difficult when my daughter came to me and
asked me whether it was true that when I was away on
business a couple of years ago I was seeing a particular lady
friend. I wanted to be honest with her about why her mum
and I separated, but I didn't want to tell her that I'd done
the wrong thing while we were still together, even though
our marriage at that time was pretty well over for me. Yet
I knew that because we'd always managed to be outwardly
fairly positive about each other and keep our disappointment
in each other private, my daughter was still trying to sort out
for herself the reasons why we couldn't be still together. If
I had told her the truth, I might have been cast as the villain
and her mother the martyr. This wouldn't have been accurate
or helpful. So I bent the truth a little bit and we had quite
a good talk about respect, companionship and the sometimes
foolish and even hurtful things grown-ups do to each other
in relationships when they don't seem to be working. It
seemed to satisfy her and I hope it left her feeling she could
talk about it some more sometime.

Perhaps even harder than answering direct questions is knowing
what line to take when you think your children are feeling a bit
torn about some aspect of 'the situation' but can't express it. There
may be times when children reflect on their circumstances and
have feelings they can't understand or express. They may tell you
about upsetting dreams, or be withdrawn and moody, or have
mystifying stomach aches. Your clue is that they seem to be
distressed out of all proportion to what they're saying the problem
is. You try to help them talk to you about what's happening to

them, and don't seem to be able to get to the bottom of it. It's frustrating because you want to help without making too much of it, but you don't want to make it worse by pressing them to explore the real issue, or worse, make them think you're defining their feelings for them, telling how they should be. Give them a few helpful pointers about likely reasons for feeling upset in a way that shows you think it's quite acceptable to feel these things, nothing to be ashamed of, and that disturbing or confused feelings are part of life. This may be enough to remind them that you understand and get them talking. Don't expect what they say to make much sense. Be reassuring, supportive and calm. Demonstrate at other times that you're happy to discuss your feelings openly too. But remember that if you're right and they are feeling churned up about someone important, it may be impossible for them to talk about this to you. Sometimes a close person outside the family can be a useful confidant.

At all costs try to keep communication channels open between you and your children. It can help them accept and even begin to understand their own feelings if they can try to express them to someone they trust. Not just feelings about divorce matters either, but about everything. Many parents are afraid to talk about emotional issues, sensitive or not, and find it hard to do this in a calm and instructive way. Men particularly can find it hard because being emotionally controlled is part of our idea of what is manly and strong. Children need parents to be able to give them emotional guidance and advice about feelings and relationships just as much as they need this about the educational, social and recreational parts of their lives. It's a great mistake to neglect this, but a rather frequent one. Children must be allowed and encouraged to express their thoughts and feelings to their family. After all, this is where they try out everything they're learning about. Then you can help them acknowledge, understand and contain their confused emotions and sometimes unnecessary anxieties in helpful and healthy ways.

To and Fro Children

In summary, here are the essential ingredients for getting the most out of the time you have with your children:

1. Show your love for them often.
2. Limit them as often as you need to, but do it consistently and respectfully.
3. Listen to them.
4. Be available for them.
5. Have fun together.

9

Reflections

You've read this book out of curiosity about your situation, to see what someone has to say about the challenges of being a parent after divorce. If you've got as far as this chapter then some of it must have made sense and struck chords. Perhaps you've said to yourself, 'OK, that's all very fine in theory, to say I should be doing this or that, or that I need to understand this feature of relationships or children's thinking or whatever. It seems to make good sense, *but how do I actually go about changing anything?*'

Changes begin with positive thinking

First of all, nothing about your life can be changed until you've acquired some new insight and understanding about the enormously complicated business of relationships, especially those in families. You won't acquire insight and understanding without there being a reason to. Your reason is whatever it was that prompted you to open this book. In that this happened, you are part way to changing your life in useful ways (whether or not you found you could identify with what you read), because something in your life prompted you to look, ask questions and think. Anybody who's willing to reflect on their circumstances in ways which acknowledge their own as well as other people's contribution to them is in effect taking charge of their life. They are emerging from the dead-end street of passively blaming events and circumstances for their sense of frustration or lack of achievement. Life involves many things that we'd rather were different, because they're hurtful, frustrating or limiting. Many of them can't be changed, and certainly the past can't be undone. Understanding the way things are, and how much you contribute to them yourself, enables you to become more accepting of people and facts. And once you have some understanding and acceptance you'll be able to let go selectively those feelings and attitudes that made you react in self-limiting ways. You'll begin to feel detached and liberated. With this comes a powerful sense of being more in charge of yourself and your life, and more able to look forward and progress in positive ways. You'll be more able to anticipate and plan your life, rather than bumble along in a random, just-about-managing kind of way.

Whether you're a mother, a father, a step-mother or a step-father, or you wear the two hats, there are aspects of a past separation that affect your daily life and thinking to some degree, which create circumstances you wouldn't wish on your children. But perhaps you can now feel this is an extension of your life, an enrichment, at least as much and hopefully more than it feels like a limitation. If you've got some way towards feeling this, you'll have given your children and step-children a very worthwhile and lasting gift. And you will have reached the necessary starting point for making real changes.

However many new perspectives you discover, you probably won't find that you're able to make the changes you want immediately. You need to reflect, discuss and consider your contribution to the way your family is, but not so that you become tentative or unauthentic or inconsistent. You'll need time to absorb new insights, share them with partner and friends, rehearse with yourself the resolutions you make, and you'll need practice. When you try them out, you probably won't manage everything you aimed for first time, so don't be discouraged. Have a post-mortem with yourself about why you didn't quite make it, and you'll get further next time. You're aiming to blend self-knowledge with having the courage of your convictions.

When there's no answer

When you find that there doesn't seem to be an answer to something that concerns you, don't despair. The fact is, there are a lot of situations that there aren't answers to, especially when you're trying to do what's best for children. But you know you'd never forgive yourself if you missed an opportunity to fix things. Quite often it isn't just that you can't find the answer, it's that there isn't one. Relationships often contain uncertainties, ambiguities, hidden agendas, grey areas, mixed feelings, and are seldom so black-and-white that clear-cut answers can be found to everything. When you've searched and thought and searched again, trying to make sense of what's going on and anticipate the probable results of whatever options you think you have, *what you must do in the end is whatever makes you feel that you're doing all you possibly can for your children under the circumstances, without compromising beliefs or values that you hold dear.*

In the period just after we separated, I was terribly concerned about what our son was going to make of it all. His Mum and I both seemed committed to presenting the decision about separating in the best way, but weren't exactly communicating with each other about it. There was this sort of defensive wall between us about the reasons we were doing it and how valid our opinions about each other were. It meant we got nowhere together over our son, though we obviously both wanted to. I didn't really understand why she wanted to split so much when her accusations about me were so unfounded; I wasn't even sure she really knew for sure that we should. So how was I going to explain it to Adrian?

I agonised about it a great deal and found I kept wanting to check with someone – and I had been talking to a counsellor – whether I'd handled my latest chat with Adrian the right way. I was looking for expert answers as if there was sure to be one. All the time I was saying to myself, 'How can I get it right when I've no idea what she's really feeling, or what she's saying to him?' Usually Adrian's response would be something like 'It's OK, Dad, don't worry about it, it's not bothering me, I can handle it, it's no big deal.' Then I'd lie awake at night wondering whether he was just trying to be brave, covering up all sorts of doubts and conflicts about it. If only I'd pitched it right he'd open up more and I'd be able to help him. Sometimes I felt quite panicky about how to do the right thing.

It didn't help that his Mum was doing what seemed to be fairly erratic things in her newly-separated life, like being out a lot and apparently spending a lot of money on herself. If only she'd see how she appeared to us – disorganised and uncertain. Adrian seemed puzzled and a bit resentful about her making him feel neglected and introducing new non-family priorities in her life at the expense of the time and attention she once had for him. It was really hard to respond to his questions about her.

After a while it started to dawn on me that there really is no perfect recipe for getting it exactly right. You can't always explain things to a child, or really know what they're thinking or feeling. You can only make a sensible guess. And it's important not to compromise the dignity and stature you have with your child and the security this offers, by sharing your own doubts and concerns too openly. It's bound to reflect on the other parent however hard you try. I think you can share some of your mixed feelings and unanswered questions in the interests of honest communication with a child old enough to have some kind of understanding, as long as you show you're coping with it all yourself (even if privately you don't think you always are!). If you show, perhaps in extra ways, that your relationship with your child is as strong and committed as ever, and they're communicating with you from time to time about what's happening in the family, then that has to be enough. I guess it probably is, and worrying too much about finding the right answer doesn't do you or the situation any good. It was quite a relief when I got the confidence to realise this!

Acceptance

You can't do much to change the way your children's other parent is. They can only change when they're ready to, and anyway, they're not likely to change at the suggestion of an ex-partner. When you don't like what you think, or know is going on in your estranged partner's life, remember that everyone is merely coping in their own way – just as you are – with the demands and challenges of family responsibilities as they see them. You have to accept the way they are, remembering that's part of why you didn't stay together. You have to use your efforts more fruitfully to think about things you could do to help your child. These are the things we've discussed like being consistently positive in the love, support and direction you give your child and your family. This way you won't be trying to battle against something that you really have no power to change. *But you do have a right to be you, and to bring up your children the way you want to when they're with you, modelling in yourself the things you'd like them to copy.*

Having doubts

You'll probably feel at sometime or other that the to and fro arrangement you've had to make for your children because of a decision you made in the past may be churning them up more than is really good for them. You may think it might be better to let a new family take over and have more of a back-seat position in their lives yourself. Or you might dwell on whether you could have tried harder to work things out in the marriage so you could have stayed together. Then you'd have avoided all you've put them through, and perhaps even been happier yourself than you find you now are. Take heart. Being positive about your children's continuing contact with both parents has many more pluses for them than minuses. No family or relationship is perfect, though sometimes you may look around wistfully at the happy-go-lucky simplicity you think you see in some marriages and families. Your children will weather the ups and downs probably better than you do. They stand to learn useful things about feelings, families and coping, things which are a very real and important part of everyday life.

Being realistic about parenting

Being a parent under any circumstances is a challenge, but because most of us are parents, it tends to be seen as something that just happens. Instinct and intuition are supposed to take care of the challenges, which are seen as normal and to be expected. Sure the challenges are normal, but they're still real and need to be faced head on. Anticipating the negative aspects of inevitable realities, and being ready for them, is in fact being positive. Some of us don't approach them very realistically, perhaps partly because we think that having children is such a usual thing for everyone that it should be a breeze. This makes it harder for us to admit that adjustments have to be made, effort put in, and that we can get it wrong, affecting how our children turn out, even disadvantaging them.

Most families are nothing like the gloriously happy, cooperative, respectful, accomplished group we aspire to. You can't change the fact that family life with a past can at times be sad, hectic, confusing, disappointing, and enraging, but then so is life in general sometimes. All the joy, fun, love, laughter and rewards of life in general can be there too, though.

We don't usually question the love we have and are always meant to feel for our children. But they are separate beings and so are bound to disappoint us sometimes, or even seem unlovable. Your children are not an extension of you, not all of what they do shows you up. They are a complex mixture of what they happened to be born like (part of which is inherited from you), and the combined effects of all they experience from the moment of conception onwards. You and your feelings are separate from your children and their feelings, and they need to be. You may find yourself wanting to attribute aspects of your children's makeup that you don't like to those parts of their experience that the other parent is responsible for. Accept these feelings in yourself but don't convey them to your children personally. They need to believe you approve of them more than they need anything else, though they must know that you cannot approve of all they do.

Some families share their children as equally as possible so neither parent feels subordinate to the other. This is a fine ideal and works well if parents get on well, and can live near each other. Certainly, whatever the arrangements, you should be aiming to make it seem that neither parent is more important than the other, and the amount of time each spends with the children needn't determine this. But it does tend to, especially in the mind of a part-time parent. There's no getting away from the fact that fathers often feel frustrated at the limitations of occasional contact with their children. It is limiting, and you have to accept this. Quite a number of fathers see less and less of their children as time goes on, because they experience these feelings of powerlessness about being a parent, and new things happen in their own lives which help old bonds weaken. While you may at times envy the amount of time your children spend with their Mum, and hence the close relationship they're able to have, she may not find this compensates for the frustrations she feels in her life. Like making all the day-to-day decisions alone, working hard to run a home for several people, missing adult companionship, earning an inadequate income, sensitively managing all the children's daily ups and downs.

Children, boys as well as girls in different ways at different times, need a male parent as well as needing the person who is their father. Despite your sense of isolation from your children's daily lives, consider that you may be able to offer them much more than you would have had you and their Mum been able to work things out together. You'll have opportunities to parent unlike those many happily married natural fathers ever have, because you've had the impetus to think about fathering, to make new and creative efforts to make the most of the time you do have with them.

Taking care of yourself

It's a mistake to neglect yourself in your efforts to be a successful parent. Don't be afraid that self-reflection and looking after your own interests is self-indulgent. Putting other people first all the time, something that committed parents, especially home-making mothers, quite often do, can sometimes make you feel frustrated, resentful, unappreciated or unfulfilled. You probably won't show it or won't think you do, perhaps because you think these feelings aren't very worthy and should be suppressed, or you aren't aware of what it is that's making you feel that your life or your marriage isn't working out quite right for you. Make sure you put yourself first sometimes, exploring the individual creativity and potential that is uniquely yours, including your talent for parenting. A good counsellor can help you explore and extend yourself in positive ways, as well as help you get over a relationship that still seems to be affecting you more than you want it to. Looking after yourself needn't mean you neglect anybody else. It can mean a more content you, less governed by other people and circumstances, with more to offer others, especially your children.

Epilogue

Look at it objectively and you'll see that sharing your child with another family becomes an issue only because of who that family is. After all, most parents like having some time without their children, and doing this can have many useful purposes, not just for you as a couple. We want our children to become independent, to part from their parents with confidence to go and have new and different adventures away from home as they grow. But however cordial your separation was and however well you have cooperated over the years as a continuing team for your children, this kind of going away from home – to home – is different.

The main difference is how much freedom you can give your children to have their own feelings, thoughts and reactions to everything about their time with you, their time without you, what they share between their two families, what happinesses and sadnesses they experience about the fact of having the two most important people in their lives in separate places.

And it's this freedom which is the most important ingredient you can provide so they get the very best of both their worlds.

I'm glad the divorce was when I was much younger. I've got used to things being the way they are and I don't remember much about it. It would be harder if you were older when it happened, I suppose. I hate the fact that my real Mum and Dad are so separate. I'm glad Dad got married and had children, even though I'm eleven now and they're a bit young for me. But they feel like brother and sister – that's nice – and they're good fun (in small doses!). Sometimes I get really mixed up about not being able to see Dad more. I have a great time when I'm staying with him, it's always lively with lots of things to do and people to see. Dad's wife is OK too, like a sort of friend who looks after the things my Mum normally does. She spoils me a bit! I can't go to Dad's as often as I'd

like because it's too far. But I think of it as my other home.
With Mum, life's a bit quieter, more routine, it's a sort of more
grown-up atmosphere. My step-father's OK, he has lots of his
own hobbies and interests. Mum takes me skiing in winter,
and we go walking a bit. I wish I had a computer. With Dad
we do a lot of waterfront things, sailing and swimming. We're
always talking about doing more modelling but there's never
enough time. I like pottering around with Dad doing jobs and
helping him at work. We send each other tapes and sometimes
home-made videos. I think I'm probably lucky to have two
homes, but I wish they weren't quite so separate.

INDEX

acceptance 151
ambivalence 94
arrangements
  commitment to 50
  discussing with children 51–3
  flexibility 48–9
authority 111–28
  family rules 113–4
  losing 115–20
  maintaining 120–8
  parental 112–3
  unity of 122–3

babies, and separation 30–2, 45, 52,
  73 *see also* children
belongings, sorting out 64
blame 35ff, 56, 68, 80–1, 142–6 *see
  also* fault
blood relationships 83–6

Children Act (1989) 9
children
  age 130–1, 135, 136
  awareness of 135–6, 144–5
  effects of divorce on 129–56
  good parenting 138–42 *see also*
    parenting
  independence 139
  loyalties 130–2
  materialism 136–7
  signs of disturbance 134
  singletons 134
  time with 138
  vulnerability 134–7, 144ff
  young children 130–1, 135–6
communication 16ff, 36, 49, 51, 55ff,
  62, 68, 93, 121, 125, 134, 138, 145

confidence 121 *see also* insecurity
custodial parent 19

decisiveness 121
detachment, importance of 126
discipline 72–4, 96, 100–1, 139
divorce
  attitudes to 16–7
  effects on children 129–56
  effects on parenting 12–3, 14,
    132–3
  'ghosts' 51
  legal term 20
doubts 151–2

fathering *see also* parenting
  communication 62–3
  compromise 62–3
  consistency 63
  discipline 72–4
  early days 61–2
  new partners 75–8
  parting 73–4
  post-divorce 14–6, 31–2, 48–50,
    61–78
  step 88–9
  treats 71–2
  using time 70–2
fault 35ff, 56, 80–1, 142–6
financial affairs 54–5

holidays 47, 65
honesty 37, 62–3

independence, of children 139
insecurity
  of children 134–7

of step parents 106–7, 121

labels, effect of 19–21, 89–91
listening, importance of 35–6, 125
loyalty, of children 130–2

mealtimes 53–4
mothering *see also* parenting
   part-time 97–110
   post-divorce 13–4

'new children' 104
new partners 75–8 *see also* step-
   relationships

'occasional parents' 61–78
occasional step-parents 97–110
older children 52, 56
only children 134
over-sensitivity 57–9, 66–9, 106–7

parenting
   aims of 11–2, 153–4
   commitment to 50
   discussing with children 51–3
   flexibility 48–9
   good 138–42
   occasional 61–78, 97–110
   part-time mothering 97–110
   positive thinking 147–8
   privacy 104
   punishment 134

questions, children's 55–6

record, keeping a 69–70
relationships
   expectations 25–6
   new 79–96
   and parenting 23–4
   and romance 24–5
replacement, fears of 77, 85, 89
resentment
   by step-mother 108

of ex-partner 13–4
of step-mother 108
role boundaries 87–9
romance 24–5
rules, in family 113–4

school holidays 47, 65
second household, establishing 44
security, children's 130–1, 135–6
separation 27–8, 43–4
   growing apart 28–30
shared parenting
   common concerns 51
   making it work 47–51
   positive approach 35–41
   reasons for 33–5, 58–9
   two-household family 43–60
shouting 123–4
singleton 134
step-families 83–96
   characteristics 83–6
   grandparents 92–3
   new babies and 91–2
   past families and 94–5
   positive steps 93–6
   responsibilities in 86–8
step-fathers 88–9
step-relationships 37, 38–9, 57, 67,
   75–8, 79–96
   timing 80–2
surnames 90–1 *see also* labels talking
   to your children 43–4

time, spending it well 70–2, 138
timing of new relationships 80–2
treats 72
two-household family 43–60
   planning 43–7

visits 45–7
   fortnightly 46–7

warnings, giving children 124